# Lost & Found

**The person I was**
**The discovery of adoption**
**The person I've become**

**by Mimi Tanaman**

## Contents

| | | |
|---|---|---|
| Prologue | | 6 |
| I | **Out of the blue** | 9 |
| | An island off the coast of New Zealand – February 4, 2008 | 9 |
| II | **It was the war** | 15 |
| | Wartime Birmingham, UK – December 1942– March 1944 | 15 |
| III | **Growing up as Michael Carlson** | 32 |
| | Birmingham, UK – 1944-1956 | 32 |
| IV | **New Zealand Bound - March 1956** | 37 |
| | Falling in love - April 1956–August 1962 | 45 |
| | Settling in | 50 |
| | The great outdoors | 53 |
| | New Zealand schooldays | 57 |
| | Disenchanted | 62 |
| V | **Back to Birmingham – August 1962– March 1964** | 65 |
| | The voyage | 65 |
| | The party's over | 69 |
| | The life of a Birmingham bachelor | 71 |
| VI | **Going home to New Zealand – March 1964** | 74 |
| | Acclimating to adulthood | 79 |
| | Learning to fly | 82 |

|      |                                                         |     |
|------|---------------------------------------------------------|-----|
|      | Fear of flying                                          | 85  |
|      | Finding my place in the work world                      | 86  |
|      | Moving up toward a downward slide                       | 87  |
|      | The second time around                                  | 89  |
|      | New work ventures                                       | 94  |
|      | Life in Fiji                                            | 96  |
|      | The rest of my life in a nutshell                       | 98  |
| VII  | **Search and discovery**                                | 99  |
|      | Looking for my mother                                   | 104 |
|      | My paternal legacy                                      | 115 |
|      | About my father                                         | 117 |
|      | Meeting my family                                       | 119 |
|      | Meeting my ancestors                                    | 121 |
|      | Dispelling all doubt                                    | 123 |
|      | Touchdown in Israel                                     | 125 |
| VIII | **The journey to Judaism – Reconnecting with my ancestral roots** | 128 |
|      | Early epiphanies                                        | 129 |
|      | Official recognition – The key to my future             | 135 |
|      | My day in court                                         | 137 |
|      | A heart-stopping glitch                                 | 138 |
|      | Living in Tztat                                         | 140 |
|      | The wedding                                             | 145 |
| IX   | **An expanding family**                                 | 146 |
|      | Horrific revelations                                    | 148 |
| X    | **From here on…**                                       | 150 |

## Prologue

*One month shy of his 64th birthday, Mike Carlson (a pseudonym) discovered that everything he thought he knew about himself and his life, the people in it and where he came from, was all a sham – and he had been deliberately misinformed. His parents were not his biological parents, nor were his brother and sisters any blood relation. Determined to discover the truth of his birth and biological heritage, Mike embarked on an investigation that took two and a half years and culminated in his uncovering a wartime romance and the reasons for his adoption, the existence of four "half siblings" and the identity of his mother whom he contacted only to be rejected once again. Having discovered his Jewish heritage from his father's side, along with a new and welcoming family stretching from England to the US and Israel, his path of discovery led him and his devoted partner Rochelle to make life changing decisions.*

*This is a true story, although names have been changed to protect people's privacy. It is the story of Mike's life, unsettled by family upheavals, of a young boy who found his own way, fell in love with a country, became disenchanted with family, established his own, and thrived on his own business initiatives from New Zealand to Fiji. Connecting with people and quickly making friends wherever he went, what he lacked was a feeling of family connectedness, of belonging. With the discovery of his adoption, a lifetime of feeling at odds suddenly made sense to him. Armed with his characteristic head-on engagement with whatever life offers up, and a proven ability to deal with adversity and come out on top, Mike was determined to digest this new information and come to terms with his true origins.*

*I am, by marriage, one of the relatives that Mike managed to locate on his father's side. Following the first email contacts and meetings over Skype, my husband and I spent time with Mike and his wife Rochelle, first at our home in Israel, then at their second home in Italy, and finally on an extended visit to their home in New Zealand. Mike mentioned that several people had said his story was so fascinating he ought to write a book. A copywriter and translator by profession, I volunteered for the job, much to Mike's excitement. Following innumerable hours of talking, going through copious lists of questions and floods of emails,*

*I've collected a collage of images, events and emotions as seen, felt and related by Mike. I've taken the liberty, with Mike's permission, of writing his story in the first person, as if Mike were speaking, telling it as he told me.*

*On hearing his story, many people have been amazed and deeply moved. But motivation for writing the book goes beyond its possible entertainment value. Mike sustained a severe shock and overcame numerous difficulties to uncover and come to terms with his true parentage and identity. There is a lesson here.*

*"If I can help just one person," Mike has said more than once, "to understand how to go about it, to persevere, discover and come to terms with their truth, then writing the book will have been worthwhile."*

*Mimi Tanaman*
*Ra'anana, Israel*

*Author's note: All the names appearing in this book have been changed to protect the privacy of the innocent and the not so innocent. All the events described in this book are based on fact as related to the author by the protagonist, and based on his research and official documentation – with the exception of the chapter "It was the war" which, while based on culled facts, was embellished with the author's imagination and presented as such in the text.*

*©2014, Mimi Tanaman, all rights reserved. The contents herein, in whole or in part, may not be copied, changed, reproduced, or made use of in any way unless by prior written permission from the author.*

# I
# Out of the blue

*It's odd that at the age of 63 I start to ask myself questions such as, who am I really? Whom do I look like? Whom do I take after? I wonder what my dad was like, or what kind of person my mother was. What kind of family background do I come from? I don't even know who my relatives are or where they are today. Would they like me? Would I like them? Would they look like me? These are basic questions that most people have solid answers to by the time they reach the age of 10. So why now? The answer is that only now, everything I thought I knew about myself and my family has been proven false. It happened out of the blue, like a thunderbolt on a clear sunny day.*

## An island off the coast of New Zealand – February 4, 2008

It was a typical February on the island. The sky was an unblemished, mid-summer blue above the deeper blue of the sea, calm and sparkling. There was a view down to the sea from the upstairs deck of our home whose natural wood exterior echoed the thick lush foliage surrounding it. On a windswept day the sound of the waves carried up the hill, but that day it was calm and quiet. A gentle balmy breeze was barely rustling the leaves, long and splindly ones, wide and oval, spiky or delicately feathered. They came in an exotic array representing the indigenous New Zealand bush. There was the huge Puriri tree with gnarled, knobby trunk and branches spreading wide. Once a year, in the dead of winter, it would delight us by becoming completely covered in a fabulous display of bright fuchsia flowers. It delighted the birds no less, for them a lifeline offering the season's only nectar-rich sustenance. And there was the Kohekohe with its broad leaves and hanging sprigs of delicate white flowers, or nut-like fruit splitting open to reveal a deep red interior. The Pohutukawa tree, another annual bloomer, would burst into a mass of bright red flowers adding color to our early summer Christmas season. Its riot of red contrasted nicely with the snowy white flowers of the giant Kanuka, whose thin feathery leaves were offset by the long green spikes of the numerous Nikau palms. Brought up in industrial Birmingham, I still got a little thrill when I surveyed the bush that we had the good fortune to call our home.

We came across the property while spending our third winter on the island, and purchased it in 1995. It was what we call a batch, a tiny bachelor's hide-away on a small island – a several hour boat ride or less than an hour's flight from mainland New Zealand. It had just two pokey little bedrooms, an upstairs lounge/dining area and a small balcony. One architect and nine months of living in miserable construction-site conditions later, we had succeeded in converting it into a comfortable three-bedroom residence with a proper kitchen and toilets – for an island dwelling, that is. Given the lack of infrastructure on the island, the house was supplied with water from collection tanks and with electricity from the eight rooftop solar panels. We liked being self-sufficient. It suited me and Rochelle down to the ground.

Rochelle, my auburn-haired, freckle-faced wife with an easy disposition and always ready cheerful chuckle, is a wonder of efficiency. Among her gardening, cooking, business management and other skills, she is an expert at packing light.

## Out of the blue

She had finished her preparations and was ready for the flight to Auckland where the plan was that she'd clean up our rental apartment, and then continue on from there to Wanaka in South Island to visit her mother. She walked down the drive to where it met the main road, the spot marked by our post box perched atop its ancient tree stump stand. It was a pleasant walk, shady with dappled sunlight, and included a wooden bridge built over the roots of the giant Pohutukawa tree. She was relieved to see the post box still in place; located as it was on a tight curve, it sometimes got collected by a passing vehicle and had to be retrieved from down the bank. She extracted the letters and, as she came back into the house sorting through the weekly mail delivery (once every five days to be precise), she called out to me, "Oh look, Mike, that's nice, you have a letter from your brother." Typically, I was busy at the computer until minutes before it was time to leave, and it was in fact fifteen minutes before our planned departure for the airport. I turned away from the screen to have a look at my letter. It wasn't often I received any communication from my brother Richard, living in Perth, Australia.

"Let's have a look," I said taking the letter. I opened it and began to read, '*It is with regret that I write this letter to you as I know that it will, of course, cause you some distress.*' My heart began to pound. What's this then? I carried on reading. '*...With* (our parents) *now dead and these documents coming to light, I feel that, even though it has taken way too long, it is time that somebody told you the facts of your adoption and gave you the documents that are rightfully yours.*' With trembling hands I thumbed the pages. There were indeed documents. And there it was, the thunderbolt out of the blue. As I read, I felt as if everything was suddenly frozen in time – my breathing, my pounding heart, my whole body momentarily going cold. And then the thin thread from which everything seemed to be suspended snapped.

"Rochelle," I said when I could breathe again, "I can't believe it. It says I'm adopted."

"What?! Let me see." There was no denying the words, or the accompanying adoption documents enclosed with the letter.

*'… I know that this will inevitably be a shock to you…'* A shock, he had no idea! *'…but I hope that you, Elisabeth and I will be able to continue our somewhat disjointed brother-sister relationship and continue to keep in touch as we have in the past. Best wishes, Richard'*

What is he saying? He's saying he's not my brother and never has been. He's offering to "continue our somewhat disjointed brother-sister relationship" even though it's a pretense. They both knew. How long have they known? They all knew except me. They all lied to me. My own mother lied to me… but no, she isn't. She wasn't really my mother. And Stan was no more my father than Rod, my mother's second husband – correction, my adoptive mother's second husband. My head began to spin. I was in the center of a vortex, a giant lie that I had thought was my family. My body responded to the emotional tumult filling my eyes with tears.

"Mike, I don't have to go to my mother now. Do you want me to stay?"

Recovering quickly, I said, "No, this is something I have to deal with myself. It's okay. You go to your mother and I have to go and photograph that property like I promised – it's a perfect day for it."

We drove to the airport with me reassuring Rochelle I'd be fine, and telling myself I had to pull myself together. I had work to do. But in truth, I was a mess. We wondered, why now? Richard had obviously known for some time, perhaps all his life, so what prompted him to finally tell me now? We had no answer, not then anyway.

After dropping Rochelle off by the small terminal building and grassy landing area designated as the island's airport, I stopped by the community center to deliver some old clothes. The island residents make up a small community and everyone knows everyone. The social worker there took one look at me and said, "Mike, you look in shock."
"I am," I told her, "I just found out I was adopted." She made suitable sounds of surprise and sympathy. We parted and I continued on to my friends' property deep in the forest. Shortly after arriving, I blurted out to them my news. "Looks like I was adopted during the war," I said. They were also shocked and tried to be comforting, offering me a welcome drink. I photographed, had a beer and set off back home.

Once at home, I became a single-minded person of action. The online Italian lessons I had been studiously working on every day since we returned from our first summer in Tuscany, were abandoned as I determined to come to grips with this new state of affairs. The first thing I did was to phone each of my children, Paul, Alex and Miriam. Phoning my eldest first, Paul, in London, I told him the news. He said flatly that he didn't believe it. "I'm going to get to the bottom of this," Paul said, "I'll go and look up the document myself." I gave him the number on the certificate of adoption Richard sent, and we agreed he'd go to Somerset House and check the documents. I knew it was true, but I needed confirmation. I couldn't help thinking how uncanny it was that we all thought Paul looked so much like my father…, correction, my adoptive father, Stan Carlson. I spoke with Alex in Auckland who also refused to believe it, and with Miriam who was in Christchurch doing a university course. She accepted the news with quiet consternation. The next thing I did was send an email to each of them attaching the scanned documents and the letter I had received from Richard, and promising I would discover who their true grandparents were.

The last thing I did that night, after another glass or two of wine, was to go into the online General Register Office in London to look up and order my original birth certificate. I found my birth registration, and a very strange feeling came over me as I looked at the name – John Robin Howard – knowing that was once me. And I knew something else. I knew that I had started on a life changing journey.

Now, after several years of painstakingly tracing documents, collecting hard evidence, tracking down scanty bits of information, I've been able to form a less than high definition picture of things I was never meant to know. Based on amassed details, from electoral roles verifying place of residence, to records of employment and military service, from family member testimonies, to documented events, I can go back to day one and begin to piece together the origins of my life, the circumstances of my parentage.

Putting together all the verifiable facts, like pieces in a puzzle, this is how I imagine it might have happened...

# II
# It was the war

## Wartime Birmingham, UK – December 1942 - March 1944

It was another one of those harrowing nights. Claudia hated being alone. She'd only been married a couple of years, but it seemed like she hardly had a chance to get used to married life when he was gone again, recruited. It had been 4 months since she'd seen him last, and then for only 4 days – special leave before being shipped overseas for active duty. Thanks a bunch. So now she not only spent the nights alone worrying about where he was and if she'd ever see him again, but she had to cope with the almost nightly air raids, too. It was hard enough getting to sleep at all, but it became near impossible when you knew you might be brutally dragged out of sleep at any moment by sirens and you'd have to rush out of bed, stick your feet into your slippers, grab a coat that would hide your nightdress to acceptable levels of propriety, and dash out to the Anderson Shelter where you'd meet the neighbors, similarly attired. The raids were such a regular occurrence that it was hardly worth getting into a night dress at all, and often, Claudia just dressed warm and waited for the sound of the siren. To avoid the late night dash, some people brought their pillows and blankets to the shelter early in the evening, along with a thermos of tea and a magazine, and settled themselves in for the night. That might be okay for families, or at least couples who could keep each other company, but not when you were a young woman on your own because your husband was god knows where fighting the war.

Nearly one and a half million of these corrugated steel shelters had been distributed during the first few months of the war. They offered no protection against a direct hit, but they were reasonably effective against shrapnel and flying debris. Neighbours helped each other dig big holes in their gardens where the thin metal shelters were half buried and covered over with dirt, which was why they were typically cold, dark and damp. And who knew what crawly things you'd encounter inside. By the time Claudia had moved in to her new home on Wheeleys Road, quite a nice area for her first abode as a married woman, the shelter was a hump in the garden with grass growing over the top. As it could accommodate up to six people, one shelter was shared by two or three households. If you were lucky, your neighbours didn't have too many children and there was room enough for everyone to sit or even lie down when it became expedient to stay for the duration of the night. Claudia considered herself lucky, as the neighbours sharing her shelter were a young couple, not yet parents. They were Jewish, but she didn't mind. They were nice enough. In fact, Claudia didn't really understand what the fuss was all about. So they went to a different place to pray and they went on a Saturday instead of a Sunday. So bloody what, she thought. They weren't any different from anyone else. People were just people as far as she was concerned.

But in fact, if truth be told she was rather pleased that particular couple were her neighbours, because she remembered him. He had worked at BSA, the Birmingham Small Arms company, as she had done, two years earlier. Production of arms was being stepped up and lots of people were hired under the Emergency Powers (Defense) Act of May 1940. The workforce had voluntarily started working a seven-day week, so everyone got to know everyone else, or at least got to be on nodding terms as they were all but living together full time. She remembered him from there. His name was Robin. She remembered the direct hits the BSA suffered in August that year. Seven-hundred and fifty machine tools were lost, but they somehow managed to escape any loss of life. Claudia remembered how Robin had been very helpful with everyone scrambling to shelters. And she remembered the smiles they had exchanged now and again. Smiles that had made her feel beautiful. The way he looked at her. She could tell he remembered too.

As for his wife, Moyra, Claudia had become quite friendly with her since they were neighbours. They were close in age, both recently married and both looking forward to the occasional visits from their uniformed husbands. That is, until Moyra's husband was de-mobbed from the RAF and became a full-time resident of their marital home, and three months later Claudia's Keith had been shipped overseas. That's when everything started to feel different. Claudia watched Robin and Moyra in the shelter. Robin's penetrating brown eyes made Claudia feel like blushing whenever they met hers, which was increasingly frequent now that they were not only neighbours and sharing a shelter, but once again working together, this time at Ridgeway's where he resumed his former occupation as head waiter and Claudia was now working as a waitress. Moyra was lucky to have him back with her. She watched Moyra lean closer to her husband with each echoed boom of a falling bomb. She wished she had someone to snuggle against in the shelter as they listened to the drone of planes overhead and the explosions around them. It was quite frightening. You never knew what you'd find the next morning, which building, shop, or neighbour's home might have been turned into a pile of rubble or a charred hole in the ground. You just hoped it wouldn't be yours.

Tonight the explosions seemed to be coming closer, getting louder. The vibrations of every impact were quite strong. Robin and Moyra were snuggled together. Claudia sat on the opposite bench. When a particularly close explosion brought dust down on them and shook the walls of the shelter, Claudia jumped up and nearly wrapped herself around Moyra. Robin protectively reached his arm round Moyra's back to include Claudia in his embrace. She felt his hand grip her shoulder and tighten reassuringly. Then his hand slowly reached up and his fingers touched the curls on the back of her neck. She felt him bury his fingers in her hair, stroke her head, outline the edge of her ear. It gave her shivers up and down her body, but at the same time made her feel flushed and warm. She wished Moyra could just disappear and she could press herself against his strong protective body. And then she caught herself.

"Claudia Faye Gates, what has got into you?" she reprimanded herself using her full maiden name as her mother always did when scolding. "Don't you forget you're a married woman now, and more to the point, so is your friend Moyra." That was her mother's voice in her head, but her own little voice answered back in a barely audible thought whisper, "Keith's been away four months now and it seems like an eternity. I hardly remember the sound of his voice, and lord knows if he'll ever be back, or if I'll still be here for that matter, what with high street stores turning into holes in the ground from one day to the next." And as a mantra-like afterthought she added, "The only certainty is now." Robin had said that one day at the restaurant. She had finished her shift and before heading home had said, "See you tomorrow." He answered with eyes looking deep into hers, "Maybe, you never know, the only certainty is now," and then he broke the moment with that broad grin of his that made you smile back and feel silly and happy for no good reason.

Claudia closed her eyes. Keenly aware of Robin's hand now back on her shoulder, she felt the warmth of Moyra's body and imagined it was Robin's warmth penetrating her. She focused on it, trying to blot out the drone of planes and the explosions

### It was the war

of the bombs. She didn't remember falling asleep, but Robin's fingers brushing her cheek woke her. It was about five in the morning, the hour when, across the city, shelters would spew out their inhabitants, groggy from a poor night's sleep, to begin another day. Still leaning against Moyra, she straightened up and Moyra, who had been slumped against Robin, did the same, like a rewind of three dominoes that had fallen over. "Sorry, Moyra, hope I didn't make you uncomfortable," Claudia apologized as she sat up rubbing her face awake. "Oh no, you helped keep me warm," Moyra answered. Robin said nothing, but his eyes met Claudia's, and she remembered the feeling of his fingers in her hair and blushed.

They clambered out of the shelter, relieved to see their homes still intact, glass windows and all.

"Bye, have a good day," Claudia called out heading toward her back door across the yard.

"You too," Moyra answered, with a tone that implied keep safe, rather than have fun.

As Robin ushered Moyra through their door he turned back to Claudia, "You're doing the second shift today aren't you?"

"Yeah," she called back nodding.

"I'll meet you out front, we can walk together," Robin said.

"Okay, thanks," Claudia answered and disappeared into the house.

Moyra looked at Robin. "That's nice of you, love," she said, "after a night like last night, it's nice to have company, especially when there might be gruesome sights along the way. That's one of the things I love about you, Robin. You're a very thoughtful person," Moyra said putting her arms around his neck as he closed the door behind them.

Robin came down the stairs from his front door just as Claudia rounded the corner.

"Good timing," she smiled as they fell into step together for their 20 minute walk to the restaurant.

Robin looked back at the house and waved to Moyra who was at the window. She smiled and waved back, and Claudia waved too. It was a scene that was to be repeated many times. Moyra would stand a while at the window watching them walk down the street together. They could easily be mistaken for a couple, she thought. Claudia was a pretty girl and she knew Robin had an eye for pretty girls. Moyra, always looking for reasonable explanations to assure herself that the world was as it should be, considered Claudia's situation. Being so young, recently married and now on her own, Claudia couldn't really be blamed for ringing their bell every time she needed a light bulb replaced that she couldn't reach, or had a leaky faucet, or, what was it the other night? That's right, it was a jar she couldn't get open. Was it getting more frequent? Robin loved being helpful, but did he seem just a little too eager? She liked Claudia. Before Robin was released from service they spent time together over tea, two young married women on their own. Perhaps it had been foolish of Moyra to have inquired about Robin getting a job at the same restaurant where Claudia worked. But it was the only one within walking distance and it seemed a good idea at the time. She had wanted to be helpful, but now she wondered. It meant her husband and Claudia were spending an awful lot of time together. There was a nagging unacknowledged worry. How far could she trust her friend Claudia, or her husband for that matter?

## It was the war

Robin and Claudia walked on in silence for a while. The air was nippy and Claudia closed her coat collar around her neck.

"Cold?" Robin asked.

"A little, just when the wind blows," Claudia answered, avoiding looking at him because she knew if their eyes met she'd see things there that excited and confused her, and her own eyes would tell him things that no respectable married woman should say. They amused each other with small talk about the cook and the other waiters and waitresses. They shook their heads at the latest piles of rubble that the day before had been habitable buildings.

As soon as they arrived at Ridgeway's restaurant, they assumed their professional roles, each busy with whatever they had to do. The hours rushed by, with just an occasional glance and smile between them, and finally it was closing time. Claudia took her time by the coat hooks until Robin appeared. It had been a while since she'd done the late shift. Had she purposely volunteered for it because it would give her a chance to walk home with him? She wasn't even sure.

"I'm a little uneasy about walking home alone in the dark what with the constant air raids," she told him.

"I wouldn't let you walk home alone," he said.

She smiled her thanks at him, and then it happened again. Their eyes met and held in a way that made her catch her breath. It almost made her dizzy. This time he broke it first and she was glad that he did. Another second and she might have swooned, or rushed into his arms. "Oh god, what's happening to me," Claudia thought. She tried to think about Keith to distract herself, or about Moyra, but her stubborn heart kept on thumping.

They stepped out into the night, oppressively dark with the blackout in effect, and she allowed him to hold her arm as they walked, although she needed no assistance. Their footsteps echoed through the mostly deserted streets. So far the skies were mercifully quiet, filled only with clouds and stars. And then suddenly he swerved into a doorway and swept her up against him. It seemed to happen in one smooth dance-like movement and they were kissing before she could think. He tasted good and his lips were soft and warm. As her excitement grew, she became frightened and pulled away. They just looked at each other for a moment and then he gently held her to him. She rested her head against his shoulder luxuriating in the relief of finally feeling him against her, the relief of the tension of wanting to be close to him, and she felt safe.

"I shouldn't feel safe," she told herself," it's all wrong," and she pushed away and blurted out, "Robin, this is not right, we mustn't."

He gathered her back in his arms and held her against him. He spoke in a whisper, with urgency, close to her ear so she could feel his warm breath on her neck.

"Claudia, you take my breath away. I can't stop thinking about you. I want you. You feel it too, I know you do. What could be so wrong about two people wanting each other?"

She had no answer, and she surrendered far too easily.

It was mad, she told herself. Spending agonizing nights in the shelter watching Robin and Moyra together. Thrilling to Robin's touch when he managed to reach out to her without Moyra's noticing. But once they were out of the house, it was as if their world consisted only of the two of them, working together, walking there and back together, and side-tracking into a bombed out building where they'd make love. It was mad, but it was also glorious.

Lyons Corner House and the adjacent Co-op were among Birmingham's many casualties of war, but in true British "carry on" spirit, the hole in the ground that had once been a popular venue for afternoon tea and a highly frequented supermarket was now converted into a huge dance floor covered by a marquis, and known as The Big Top. It had become a favorite haunt of the troops, and a place where people could go to get out of the house, out of the shelter, to forget for a little while the sleepless nights, the constant threat and fear. It was Moyra actually, who suggested to Robin that a night out might do them good. It would certainly do her good, cooped up in the house most of the time, and she wanted an excuse to dress up and look nice for Robin. It was quite out of character for Moyra to suggest going out dancing, but the options were few and the need to break routine and release tension was strong. And anyway, it was wartime. War had a lot to answer for – normal codes of behavior didn't apply anymore. Married women did the unheard of and went out to work, young boys and girls stayed up all night on fire watch or manning telephones, and young women went along to music halls to dance with perfect strangers just to help raise the morale and make 'now' a happy moment. Increasing numbers of young women whose husbands were away fighting the war found themselves alone, while increasing numbers of male recruits, feeling displaced and far from home, were all too eager to alleviate their loneliness.

"You don't mind, love if we take Claudia along with us," Robin said as they were getting ready to go out. "Poor thing is on her own every night."

Moyra's heart sank. "Is there no end to your thoughtfulness," she replied with just a hint of sarcasm. "As long as you two don't go dancing off and leave me standing. You're my dance partner tonight and don't forget it!" Moyra said laughing.

They went early evening, so they could get back home before it got very late, hopefully before the inevitable night air raids. Claudia was careful to avoid meeting Robin's eyes. She tucked her arm around Moyra's and they walked together like two girlfriends. They could hear the band playing as they approached the marquis, and as they entered, the sudden light, noise and gaiety washed over them like spring rain in the desert.

Against the backdrop of air raids, uncertainty and barely concealed tension, the gaiety inside The Big Top was that much more intense, boisterous, even edging near hysteria. It was like a place where you stock up on vital supplies because you don't know when you'll have access to them again. Only here the vital supplies were what you brought with you and traded with those around you. Everyone tried to exude as much jolly feeling as they could and soak up each other's to wrap round themselves like a protective coat against the next air raid, the next bit of bad news. No bad news in here. It was a magic marquis of respite.

Robin brought his ladies a drink and the three of them sipped and soaked up the atmosphere, watching the dancers. Finally, at Moyra's urging and Claudia's encouragement, Robin guided Moyra into the flow of bodies on the dance floor. Claudia stood alone watching them, but it didn't take long before she was approached by a GI and they joined the gliding, whirling couples. It was great fun. Claudia's partner was a good dancer, even if he held her a little too close. Every once in a while she and Robin gave each other knowing smiles over the shoulders of their partners.

Claudia's GI seemed in no hurry to leave her. They danced, they laughed, they were breathless, they drank, and they danced some more. Claudia allowed herself to push back the feeling that this was all a little bit naughty, because it was, after all, today's norm. You were doing your bit for the war, for the morale of the troops, by spreading a little happiness and how could you be blamed if you absorbed some yourself along the way? Finally, Robin danced over to them and cut in. Switching partners, he grasped Claudia to him and allowed Moyra to be swept up by the GI.

"I hate seeing you so happy in someone else's arms," Robin whispered into her ear.

"Well, why don't you just focus on dancing with your wife," Claudia retorted.

"I love you Claudia," he whispered back, and before she could think of replying he broke their dancer's embrace, grabbed Moyra from the arms of the GI, and said, "I think it's time we were heading home, ladies."

The next day, on the way home from work, their lovemaking was more intense, as if neither of them could bear to let go.

"Is it my imagination, or are you putting on weight?" Robin asked as he stroked her body and noticed the gentle curve of her tummy.

"I am," she said, "but it's not from eating too much."

"What do you mean?" Robin lifted his head to look at her and as the question was out of his mouth, he knew exactly what she meant. They stared at each other for a moment, and then Claudia's face began to crumple, and she buried her head in his chest as she burst into tears.

"I don't know what to do," her words came out in spurts, between sobs, "I love the thought of something of you inside me, of a baby growing in me, but what about my marriage. What do I do about Keith? I don't know what to do!"

Robin's mind raced with possibilities. Divorcing Moyra and marrying a shikse, that would really please his family! And how could he do such a thing to Moyra? She didn't deserve it. Abortion, if she wasn't too far gone, and if she'd agree, but it was expensive and dangerous. Maybe her husband could get leave and they could pass it off as his. Robin closed his eyes. He knew there was no good option. He'd run headlong into a dead end. The only thing he could do was stick his head in the sand, pretend it had nothing to do with him and carry on with his life. And whatever the consequences were, he knew he deserved every bit of it.

"The only certainty is now," Claudia now held onto that phrase with pathological devotion, because thinking ahead became far too complicated and frightening. She lived one day at a time. And as her belly began to swell she could only focus on the excitement of the new life inside her. Because thinking of anything else just made her feel physically ill.

Her husband's aunt had seen her come out of the restaurant one evening, her arm easily resting on Robin's. She had made inquiries as to who he was. It got back to Claudia's mother.

"Claudia's seeing a Jew-boy."

Claudia's mother could hear those words reverberating in her head. That woman could always be trusted to say just whatever she pleased, sparing no one's feelings, Claudia's mother thought to herself. It wouldn't do. Even if something happened, heaven forbid, to Claudia's husband and he never returned – a Jew was not an option, even if she was carrying his child, to say nothing of the fact that he also happened to be married.

"Claudia, what are we going to do with you?" her mother said to herself for the umpteenth time, and had been saying to herself these last months. "I thought marrying you off at 18 would keep you out of trouble, but now you've gone and courted even worse trouble than I'd ever considered."

As the months wore on, it became increasingly clear that Claudia was not simply putting on weight. Moyra stared and stared until she was satisfied she knew what she saw. She asked Robin, trying to sound casual, if Claudia had been seeing anyone from the restaurant, and shared with him her suspicions about her condition. But in the deep painful hollow of her heart, she knew. Robin claimed ignorance of the whole matter, until it became so very clear that they finally had it out in one screaming argument, and Moyra was gone – emotionally from the relationship if not yet physically from their home. At the restaurant it was common knowledge, although everyone tried to be discreet, or nearly everyone.

"Someone's written to Keith," Claudia told Robin as they walked home together, which they still did from the restaurant, although they'd part ways before nearing the street they lived on. "He wrote that he's considering what to do. Maybe he'll want a divorce. Oh, why is life so complicated?"

"Moyra and I had a huge row as well," Robin added.

"What are we going to do?" It was almost a rhetorical question that Claudia often repeated, wishing he'd propose some solution where they would go off together into the sunset and everyone would live happily ever after. But she didn't really expect an answer. She didn't even want an answer because she knew there was no answer. Whatever happened now, no one would experience any "happily ever after." It would all be wrong. It would involve upset and unhappiness no matter what the outcome. This she knew, and when she allowed those thoughts in, she brooded.

Always knowing how to distract her from her dark moods, Robin put a hand on her hard round belly. "How's the baby?"

Immediately brightening up, she smiled at him. "He kicks and twists so much he keeps me up at night. I'm sure it's a boy, the way he kicks!" she laughed.

"My dad's name is Jonathan, but everyone calls him John. You know that we usually name a child after the grandparent. Would you do that for me?"

"Of course, love. I like the name John. And his middle name will be for you, Robin."

"If you like," he said. "And whatever happens, he'll be ours, he'll be carrying our names."

"I don't want to think about 'whatever happens'. I don't know what will happen. I can't picture it. I can't think past now, and you."

Again, trying to cheer her up, Robin whispered in her ear, "Claudia, I love you. You're my girl. Remember that. This is where we go separate ways. I'll see you tomorrow at work."

She held him tight and finally loosened her grip. "Alright, g'bye love."

But "tomorrow at work" never came. When Claudia got home her mother was there waiting for her.

## It was the war

"Look at you," she said, "you're big as a cow about to calve. You're not going to work anymore. You don't want to start in the middle of a restaurant, do you? And you can't stay alone, either. Pack some things. You're coming home with me." And because Claudia had no plan of her own and no viable alternative, she surrendered to her mother's will.

Another letter arrived from Keith. Although his ultimatum made Claudia feel sick in the pit of her stomach, she had to admit that he really was being quite forgiving and reasonable. Considering the years of his absence, he wrote, the circumstances of the war and so on, he was willing to continue their married life when he finally returned to the UK, on condition that the child be given up for adoption, and no more would be said about it (i).

"And that's exactly what you'll do," Claudia's mother told her. "After it's born, you will tell the authorities that you wish to submit the child for adoption in order to save your marriage." She received no argument from her daughter.

---

On 18 March 1944 a baby boy was born in Sorrento Hospital, Birmingham. His given name was John Robin Howard. The birth was registered by his mother, Claudia Faye Howard. The father was not named on the birth certificate.

After mothering her firstborn child (ii) for two months, Claudia Faye Howard bathed her baby in front of the fire one last time, asked her little sister to accompany her to the office (iii), and gave him up for adoption. Over a year later, Claudia's mother, aware that her daughter was still upset over giving away her child, tried to put an end to it by telling her daughter that the now 18-month-old child had died of diphtheria (iv). In fact, the child was alive and well and living in Birmingham a short distance away, in the home of his adoptive parents, Rose and Stanley Carlson.

On 3 September 1943, just 6 months before the birth of John Robin Howard, Rose Carlson gave birth to her second son, George Carlson, who died three days later. To help overcome their loss, the Carlsons decided to adopt and shortly after the birth of John Robin Howard, they were informed of his availability. At two months old, John Robin Howard was delivered into the care of the Carlsons.

Shortly after the arrival of the adopted baby, the Carlsons held a family meeting at the home of the maternal grandfather. It included Stan and Rose, the adoptive parents, Rose's sister and brother, and her father. The patriarch of the family swore everyone to secrecy regarding the death of George Carlson and the subsequent adoption (v).

On 12 October 1944, an official adoption order was registered. It included the child's name change from John Robin Howard to Michael Carlson.

On 3 July 1945 Keith Broderick Howard returned home from active duty overseas to find his wife, Claudia, pregnant once again from a new partner (her employer at the restaurant). He subsequently enlisted for the British Occupation Forces in Palestine where he served until the departure of the British troops and the Declaration of the State of Israel (vi).

In August 1945, Claudia Faye Howard moved to London.

On 15 April 1948 Moyra Jacobs nee Solomon boarded The Queen Mary and departed for an extended stay in New York.

## It was the war

Between 1945 and 1948, the name Robin Daniel Jacobs appeared on two divorce petitions registered in Birmingham. One was brought by his wife Moyra Jacobs, and the other was brought by Keith Broderick Howard against his wife Claudia Faye Howard. In both, Robin Daniel Jacobs was named as respondent/co-respondent. In both, the grounds for divorce were adultery.

The baby that was born John Robin Howard changed hands, was registered as Michael Carlson, and his original identity and parentage were intentionally concealed and effectively erased.

---

*(i) Claudia would later be interviewed by the authorities when she applied to have the child adopted. The following is taken from the City of Birmingham Report under the Adoption Act of 1926, dated 10th October 1944. "Mrs. (Howard) says that her husband desires to continue to reside with her on his return home, and she thinks that adoption will ensure this condition being brought about and maintained."*

*(ii) Following here the sequence of my discoveries, the assumption of this being her first born would be later qualified.*

*(iii) When I made contact with my biological mother's younger sister, Patricia, in early 2013, she related that the night before the adoption I was given a bath in front of the fire and the next morning Claudia asked her to carry her son into Birmingham with her so that her baby could be handed over.*

*(iv) Reported to me in conversation with Margaret, Claudia's daughter.*

*(v) As told to me by Rose's brother, Sam Frank, in February 2008.*

*(vi) Keith Howard was, I was later to discover, my idea of a perfect WW2 British hero, a medic in a crack parachute division, evacuated from the Dunkirk Beaches in 1940, and who continued to do his duty until the end of the war in 1945.*

# III
# Growing up as Michael Carlson

## Birmingham, UK – 1944-1956

My first family, as far as I ever knew, consisted of a mother called Rose, a father called Stan, and a brother called Richard. However, very soon after my arrival, within a few months of finalization of the adoption order in fact, the family disintegrated. Apparently Rod, the best man at their wedding, became Rose's best man after the wedding, with Stan's suspicions confirmed by a detective. Stan left just months before my first birthday, taking four-year-old Richard with him. So the first family I remember was just me and Rose, and the nursery school, since she had to work to support us. The earliest evidence of my attendance there was a photograph I remember seeing of two-and-a-half-year-old me, with the date September 1946 written on the back. I guess I liked being with kids my own age, at least I don't recall any problem about going there. The only thing I really remember was the enforced afternoon nap when all the children were supposed to sleep on demand. I never did like being told what to do.

I started travelling on my own quite early in life. I can recall three occasions during the days of my attendance at nursery school, when I boarded a train to Exmouth to spend a few days with my father, Stan, and brother, Richard. I travelled there with my mother, and once with someone who dropped me off. On the return trip I was on my own, although I suppose at the age of three there must have been someone who was told to keep an eye on me. I've been asked what the greetings with my father were like, or the partings – did we hug? Was I kissed? Search my memory as I may, I don't recall any demonstrations of affection.

Upon my return from one of these visits, there were two people at Snowhill Station to meet me, my mother and some man I'd never seen before. That was Rod. They'd apparently married, honeymooned and began living together in the few days I was away. He was introduced as Uncle Rod and we simply all went home together. No one was very big on talking or explaining to a person whose age was three and three months, and I just accepted whatever reality I was presented with. From then on Rose, who was a qualified dressmaker, worked from home. For many years she specialized in creating dresses and costumes for pantomimes, which afforded me my first glimpse of the fair sex. A stream of attractive young ladies traipsed through the house, arriving for fittings or picking up their new wardrobe.

Stan came to see me once in Birmingham. The first I knew of it was when Rose came to me and said, "Your father's in the lounge waiting to see you." She might as well have said the king is requesting an audience. Stan and Richard were an unobtainable exclusive club that I only got to peer at now and again. I sat with my father in the lounge for about an hour, and I showed him a model airplane I had been trying to build. He was a stranger to me, but I remember his being very kind. Then the hour was up and his exalted personage was once again removed from my home and my presence.

Shortly after Rose and Rodney married, we moved home from Wilton Road, to Grove Lane, both in Handsworth. Rod's brother lived next door. Birmingham in the 50s was a dump. It was bleak and grey, covered with the unsightly scars of war, and it still bore evidence of its early rapid growth as an industrial center, magnet to the poor, the rural and the unemployed. People still lived in back-to-backs, the unique construction thrown up in the 1800s to house the influx of job seekers. A genuine remnant from the past, the back-to-backs were dark and airless, narrow homes built around a communal courtyard. They were generally three storeys high, with one room on each floor. The ground floor of the fronts facing the street often became shops, while the backs, accessible from the street through narrow tunnel-like passages, faced the courtyard which was used for cooking, washing and hanging laundry, as a children's play area, and as the location of rubbish bins and outhouses. The last of the back-to-backs were declared unfit for living in 1966 and demolished, although a few have been preserved as a museum. In the 50s, not yet deemed unfit for living, nor yet revered as a view of the past, the back-to-backs were just a pokey place to live, with a courtyard that was now unkempt and neglected. According to a 1911 census, my biological father and grandparents lived in a back-to-back on Gooch Street where, in fact, my grandfather ended his days in 1945. But I wasn't to know that until a lifetime later. Our own residence was only a small step up in the living standard scales.

Our house had a green door that opened onto a dark narrow hallway. On the right was the lounge, further down a staircase, and another small room which was the kitchen and dining area. Upstairs were three bedrooms and a bathroom. Above that was an attic where I sometimes played. I kept my train set up there. It was up in the attic that once, when I was about 10 years old, I opened a box of my mother's and found documents indicating that I had a brother who had died. Curious, I went to the local cemetery to find his tombstone, which may seem an odd thing for a ten-year-old boy to do on his own, but that was always like me – asking no questions, offered no answers, just going off on my own quests. I never did manage to find the tombstone. Thinking back though, I must have seen that his birth date was just 6 months before mine. If I had known anything about human biology, I would have understood then that I was adopted.

A new member joined the family when I was six. Rose and Rod had a daughter, Susan. I remember the excitement in the household over the impending arrival. I had no problem with there being a new baby in the house, but it reinforced my feeling of being an outsider. Susan slept in Rose and Rod's bedroom. It was another closed club. After all, both Rose and Rod were Susan's natural parents, while Rod was only my "uncle".

A highlight of my childhood in Birmingham was the year that Richard came to live with us – the prince from that exclusive father-son club. I was about eight, Susan two, and Richard was twelve. From April 1952 to June 1953 Richard and I shared a room and I was thoroughly pleased to have a big brother to look up to. It was during his stay that I was given to understand by Richard that Rod was to blame for the breakup of our family. So from that time on, whatever affection I may have felt for the only father I really knew, was now deemed to be misplaced and instead I bore him quite a lot of resentment.

Meanwhile Stan, my estranged father, had gone off to Australia and then New Zealand. His plan was to establish himself and then call for his son Richard to join him. By the time Richard was on his way to New Zealand, Stan was established indeed, having met and married Carole who, soon after Richard's arrival, conceived their daughter, Elisabeth.

The day Richard left us for New Zealand, my mother and I accompanied him to London and saw him off at the railway station. The city was gaily dressed for the coronation. Red, white and blue was everywhere you looked, waving at you from a riot of flags and streamers, with a bit of gold thrown in from the oft repeated decorative theme of crowns. Our sad little party stood in stark contrast to the festive mood around us. My mother burst into tears as we waved goodbye, saying, "I'll never see Richard again." I wanted to say, don't cry Mum, I'm here with you, but I knew I was little consolation for losing Richard forever.

So life in Birmingham was back to its dreary routine. I didn't like school, and I didn't do very well. Rose and Rod had hoped I'd pass the 11+, but I let them down. They never got involved with my school work, but it wasn't out of lack of interest. They were just too busy surviving – Rose at the sewing machine and Rod as a travelling salesman. I spent my time after school playing with friends in Handsworth Park opposite our house. I had no idea what I wanted to do when I grew up, but I had a pretty good idea I didn't want to do it in Birmingham.

# IV
# New Zealand bound - March 1956

A momentous letter arrived from his majesty, my father. My mother came to me, letter in hand and said, "Your father has called for you to come and live with him in New Zealand. Would you like to go?"

Wow, I thought, wouldn't that be something to tell my friends – a journey to the other side of the world! Other thoughts floating through my mind, perhaps even unawares, were that New Zealand was something far away and exotic, and being far from Birmingham, it had to be better. And here was an invitation to join the exclusive father-son club. Maybe there I'd fit in, I'd feel like a full member. And whatever else happened there, I'd be with my brother. Looking at my mother I asked her, "What about you?" She made some dismissive reply, and so without too much discussion, the decision was taken. I felt quite sad about it, about leaving her. I was excited and upset at the same time. Many years later, when Susan asked her mother why she let her sons go, she replied, "To give them a better life." She wasn't wrong there.

And I must add in hindsight, I appreciate that my adoptive father was a good man. Here he was in a new country, with a new wife and their baby daughter, when he called for Richard, and later myself, to join him. I will always be grateful for his introducing me to New Zealand.

## Lost & Found

I packed everything I owned, including my train set, as if I was never coming back. It all fit into a small leather suitcase. My passage was secured on the SS Captain Hobson departing Glasgow on March 2, 1956, and heading for Wellington via the Panama Canal. Among the 500 plus émigrés making the journey to New Zealand was a passenger travelling with his wife and children. He was designated as my escort. At eleven years old and the only child traveling without his family, I was to be the youngest solo passenger on board.

My mother and I made our way to Glasgow. Once there, she wanted to phone Rod to reassure him we'd arrived safely. We went into a pub for her to use the phone, and I'll never forget the scene that affronted my eyes and nose. It was nine o'clock in the morning, and the place was full of drunks. Even as a young boy, that much was clear to me. The place reeked of it. They were all drinking beer with whiskey chasers and the barman kept topping them up. As I took it all in, going far away seemed to me a very good idea indeed.

The harbor in Glasgow was a bustling place. The ship loomed above us looking huge and I couldn't quite believe I'd soon be on it. It was all tremendously exciting. At the dock, we met the man who was to be my escort. We exchanged introductions and niceties, and then the ship sounded its horn whose deep tones reverberated in my chest making me wonder if it was the horn or the pounding of my heart that caused a lump to form in my throat.

The man turned to me. "Say goodbye to your mother," and that's when it finally hit me. I was leaving my mother. I was leaving behind everything I knew. I didn't know where I was going. I knew nothing about it. I only knew I was going far away, into the unknown, alone.

## New Zealand bound - March 1956

I obediently said, "Goodbye Mum," and headed to the gangplank in a flood of tears. I couldn't help it. I stood on the deck, inconsolable, and watched my mother wave goodbye. I could feel the vibration of the engines in the soles of my feet as the ship's great black body heaved itself into motion and slowly began to move away from the dock.

My escort gave me an apple. "Eat your apple," he said, "and be quiet." I tried to chew the apple between sobs, watching my mother grow smaller on the dock. Eventually, chewing won out over crying.

Once I got over the shock of separation, I was filled with the exhilaration of all that was new – life onboard a ship, huge expanses of sea, the smell of salty air, the rushing sound of the wind and the waves. The voyage was a fantastic, mind-opening experience. There was a sense of freedom I'd never experienced before. I felt terribly grown up. For a full six weeks, I did as I pleased all day, every day. I shared a cabin with four older teenagers, and I was almost one of them – almost. It was becoming a life theme, being once removed from genuine belonging.

Our small cabin, located on a lower deck, had three-tiered bunk beds. Mine was on top. My escort had a cabin on an upper deck with his wife and small children. I only saw them at mealtimes when I would join him and his family at their table for the family seating. The second mealtime shift was for the singles.

The first day out, crossing the Irish channel was dreadful. The sea was rough and nearly everyone was sick. I didn't fare too badly, all things considered, and after that we headed south where the sea and the weather were calmer. Within about a week I had my sea legs and felt fine. There was always something going on up on deck, always something to do. There were organized activities and deck games, or special events such as "Guess Where on the Map We Are," with prizes for those who got it right. I also spent time reading. In Birmingham I had seen a newsreel showing Nazi bulldozers pushing dead Jewish bodies into a mass grave. When I saw one of the friends of my escort, a guy in his 20s, reading the book *The Scourge of the Swastika*, I asked if I could borrow it to read when he finished.

"You're too young to read this book," he told me.

"Well I'd like to read it," I replied.
When he put it down I took it and began to read. It was a chronicle of Nazi war crimes. I couldn't put it down and read it through to the end. Perhaps he had been right. I had nightmares for ages after that (vii).

In general, I spent my days running around the ship, and evenings we all went to bed quite early. The people on board were all kind and friendly, but I don't recall any particular friend.

The Atlantic crossing was fairly uneventful, other than sightings of whales and one breakdown during which the crew all came up on deck to do some fishing till the engines could be started up again. After about three weeks, we had completed the crossing and bid farewell to the Atlantic as we headed into the southern Caribbean.

Our first stop was Curacao, a Dutch West Indies island country off the coast of Venezuela. We docked in the harbor at Willemstad, the capital city, and were allowed to disembark, which I did together with my escort and his friends, all in their 20s. It was what I'd call a bongo town, or at least that was my impression of the area we got to see around the port – it was tropical, rundown, crowded and noisy. I remember my escort

## New Zealand bound - March 1956

bought me a game there as a birthday present. We stayed long enough for the ship to refuel and replenish its stocks, which took a couple of days. I was glad we weren't stopping there long. It looked to me even worse than Birmingham.

Our next land encounter was an entirely different experience. As we approached Cristobal Port, the eastern entrance to the Panama Canal, the captain told us the story of the building of the canal.

"Ladies and gentleman," he began dramatically, "do you see that canal that goes nowhere and ends in thick jungle…"

He told us about the French developer, Ferdinand de Lesseps, who began work on the canal in 1880. Unprepared for the conditions he was to face, he was plagued with landslides, rusting equipment, malaria and yellow fever. In 1893, after 13 years of battling obstacles, he finally abandoned the project, which was later to be picked up by others and eventually completed in 1914. Lesseps' canal, the gash he managed to inflict on the landscape, was an aimless ribbon of water punctuated by a wall of green. I'll never forget the image of that manmade canal, dug with such effort, only to become a dead end. That left a deep impression on me. All that work, and in the end nothing. Perhaps that was the origin of my dogged persistence in life, never stopping until I got results from work invested.

We traversed Panama from Colon to Panama City, stopping at the two ports, Crystobal in the Caribbean and Balboa on the Pacific coast. The sight of moving through the locks of the canal is clearly etched on my memory. Little trains, called mules, rode on rollercoaster-like tracks along each side of the narrow passage, pulling the ship into a lock. The gates would close behind us and the water would start to rise. When the water reached the designated level, the gates in front of us opened and the mules would pull the ship into the next lock. I stood on deck and watched as the water level, and the entire ship with us on it, rose high above the level of the water behind us, or fell again, depositing us back at sea level on the Pacific side. What an amazing feat of human ingenuity. It left me breathless with wonder and excitement.

Once through the canal, we were into the Pacific where, true to its name, the sea was calm and beautiful. Staring out over the expanse of blue, there were many occasions when here in the Pacific, as during the Atlantic crossing, I was treated to the sight of pods of whales, their shiny bodies and impressive tailfins rolling in and out of the waves.

Another Atlantic experience to be repeated in the Pacific was the ship's breaking down. Having been in service since 1920, taken part in wars, suffered air attack, been converted to a military hospital with over 500 beds, made countless runs to Rangoon, Hong Kong, Australia, New Zealand and back, it seems the Captain Hobson was beginning to feel its age and battle scars. Nonetheless, slow but steady, other than these two minor breakdowns, the ship faithfully carried us to our destination.

Crossing the equator was a gala event. The crew turned it into a theatrical production with one of the members dressed as Neptune, God of the Seas. Every passenger on the ship was ceremoniously presented with a certificate, signed by Neptune himself, stating that they had crossed the equator and been granted free passage throughout the seas.

And then there was Pitcairn Island.

After about 20 days with nothing on the horizon but water in every direction, there was great excitement when land was sighted. One of the passengers called out, "Look, there's an

## New Zealand bound - March 1956

island on the horizon." The news spread fast and passengers quickly gathered on the deck to see the sight, the tiny deviation on the otherwise unbroken blue horizon all around us. The only land we would pass from South America to New Zealand, and located about midway between the two, Pitcairn Island had been a topic of conversation among the ship's passengers. At age 12, I hadn't yet read *Mutiny on the Bounty*, so my source of information was what I picked up from the passengers, and it made my heart quicken to think we would be seeing the island hideaway of the legendary mutineers and perhaps even see their descendants.

For the rest of the day, the spot on the horizon slowly grew. By the time we were close enough to have discerned its landscape, there was no longer enough light to see anything more than a large ragged black silhouette against the slightly less dense black of the sky. In the dark of night we dropped anchor off this tiny island that had no port, and then began the evening's enchantment. The water was black velvet studded with sparkles, like handfuls of sequins tossed by the ship's lights. The gentle sound of oars dipping in and out of the water floated across the still night. Then a new and haunting sound was added as the islanders, approaching the ship in their longboats, began to sing hymns as they rowed, their voices suspended in the night air. The breeze was quiet, as if it too was listening to the swelling sound of song. It came out of the darkness, disembodied voices rising in unison from their numerous boats and offset by the rhythm of the oars and the gentle sounds of the water. It was the most magically beautiful sound I'd ever heard.

They entered the pool of light thrown by the ship's lanterns, about a dozen longboats, each with eight or ten oarsmen. As the boats came level with the ship, our crew lowered ladders over the side and the islanders climbed aboard bearing their crafts and wares. They were a tall people, looking as much British as

Polynesian, and spoke an antiquated English. I made my only purchase of the journey and bought a flying fish carved from drift wood. The man who sold it to me claimed to be a direct descendent of Fletcher Christian, and in fact his artist's signature – with the surname, Christian – was carved into the driftwood fish. The wide wonder in my eyes was evidence of my utter belief in his claim. Of the island's 60 inhabitants, no less than 51 claim direct descent from the famous mutineer.

After just three or four hours, the islanders departed and the ship pulled up anchor. That was our last stop before reaching our final destination, the New Zealand port of Wellington.

Some of the passengers took up the Captain's challenge to be the first to catch sight of New Zealand and win a prize. After countless more days of endless blue, and a total voyage time of six weeks, the shout finally came on April 16th.

"I can see New Zealand," one of the more vigilant passengers called out.

Everyone rushed to the side of the ship. Squinting hard and concentrating our focus, we could now all see it on the horizon. The excitement of the moment started in my stomach, accelerated my heart and welled up into my throat. Here it was, my new home, the culmination of this very long voyage, a place I was laying my eyes on for the very first time. I had absolutely no preconceptions of what I would see. I was open to just take it all in. I felt a sense of destiny, and strangely, I had a strong feeling that this scene would be repeated. Mixed with the excitement of arrival, I also felt a deep sadness. The voyage was over. For six weeks I had been my own boss and I felt very grown up. I realized I'd have to give that up now and become someone's child again.

---

New Zealand bound - March 1956

*(vii) Much later I found out that in the mid 1930's Stan had joined the Black Shirts and, wearing their Nazi uniform, had marched in Birmingham with the supporters of Sir Oswald Mosely. In the summer of 1939 he even visited Nazi Germany, but was disillusioned with his heroes when he experienced an unpleasant incident with a group of Hitler Youth, narrowly escaping their aggression.*

# Falling in love – April 1956–August 1962

Coming from crowded, industrial, war-scarred Birmingham, and having set out from the teeming city of Glasgow, I couldn't possibly have imagined the sight that New Zealand now spread before me. As we sailed along the coast I stared in amazement at its desolate hills, everywhere green. It all seemed to be covered with forest, although not the image that the word "forest" generally conjured up. This was a forest of a different kind, thick with exotic trees and bushes I'd never seen before. We approached Port Nicholas in Wellington Harbor, surrounded by its lush mountains and hills. I thought this must be the most beautiful harbor in the world. Slowly, the landscape came into sharper focus, revealing the odd house or two scattered here and there across the hillside.

The ship's passengers, all émigrés from the UK's bustling cities, began to ask in confusion, "Where is everyone?" "Where do they live?" "Is this it?"

The entire population of New Zealand at the time was only 2.2 million in an area roughly the size of the British Isles, whose population was 51.2 million.

Once the ship moored, still a little way from the harbor, a small boat set out from the shore and we were boarded by a group of government officials – immigration officers, representatives of the Bank of New Zealand, and army conscription officers. They set up a make-shift bank on the deck so that the new arrivals could change their money before disembarking.

I took my place among the adults in the queue, money in hand. When I left the UK my mother had given me a pound note saying, "Whatever you do, don't spend it before you arrive". Now I stepped up to the makeshift bank counter, which was well above my head, reached up and plunked down my pound note. The man behind the counter leaned over to have a look at the owner of the small hand. He gave me a little smile, took my note and gave me in exchange a New Zealand pound note, plus 6 pence. I looked at what I had received back and couldn't believe my luck. I was getting back even more than I'd given, and I thought, "This is a wonderful place!"

After officialdom had accomplished their various tasks, the ship approached the harbor's shoreline and lowered its gangplank. I looked down at the small group of people at the water's edge. I could count on one hand the number of times in my life I'd ever seen my father, and I hadn't seen my brother in two years. I didn't recognize anyone. A man walked up the gangplank and I realized he was coming toward me. He smiled at me and then he asked, "Where's your suitcase?" In all the excitement of the arrival, I hadn't thought to bring it up on deck. My fellow passengers of the last six weeks trickled down the gangplank to be absorbed into their newly adopted country, while I went down to my cabin to get my case. As a result, I didn't get a chance to say goodbye to my cabin mates, which caused me some regret. I experienced human connection dissolving away into nothing – a feeling, it seems, that was to be echoed later in life.

We walked down the gangplank, my father and I. Waiting a few steps away was Richard in his school uniform, my father's wife, Carole, and their daughter Elisabeth, who sat in a push

## New Zealand bound - March 1956

chair. Richard and I said hello to each other. I was quite excited about being reunited with my big brother who featured in the favorite year of my life to date, the year we had lived together. I looked up to him with great affection and awe and with the confidence that even if things don't go well, at least I'll be with my big brother; I'll have someone on my team. After our brief hello, Richard, who had been allowed time off for my arrival, headed back to the school he attended in Wellington. Carole said hello and leaned toward two-year-old Elisabeth, saying to her in sweet tones I was to discover were reserved for her alone, "Say hello." Elisabeth just looked at me. There was no hugging or kissing, or even a handshake. I was matter-of-factly taken in as a new member of the group and we walked off toward the train station.

Our home was in Pukerua Bay, 30 miles from Wellington. Stan and Richard commuted to Wellington by train every day, as I would be doing the following year to attend school. We walked to Wellington station and boarded the train for our hour and a quarter journey. Time flew by as fast as the scenery. There was so much to see in this new place and my eyes never left the landscapes gliding past the window. Even the smell of the air was foreign to me, and wonderful. It was fresh and crisp, slightly salted from the sea and heavily scented with the perfumes of the exotic bush.

At the station's little platform, I got my first glimpse of Pukerua Bay. I was overwhelmed as I looked out across the glistening sea below, the scattering of houses along the twin slopes, the thick vegetation of the surrounding hills. If anything could express my feelings at that moment, it might be a 300-voice choir accompanied by full orchestration breaking into "Love is a Many Splendid Thing." At twelve years old, I was hit by love at first sight and Pukerua Bay became my first love affair. It was beautiful beyond comprehension. And compared to the grey, war-scarred place I'd come from, it was truly a paradise.

I couldn't have imagined a better place to grow up. Being enveloped in lush nature produced in me a feeling of wellbeing. Within a few weeks I was totally involved in my surroundings. There were sparkling beaches for swimming or lazing in the sand, and clear waters occasionally visited by dolphins or whales. There was fishing, with colonies of crayfish just waiting to be lifted out of the shallow waters. And there was the wildlife, bush and forest to muck about in and explore. My favorite area was called 100 Acre Bush because it was approximately 100 acres of indigenous and ancient native forest. There were tall trees and dense coverage making the ground cool and dark even during the day, but it was not a foreboding place. It was a wonderland.

In Maori, Pukerua, or puke rua, literally means two hills, and the name described the village built on the slopes between the hills. There was nothing flat about the place. Wherever you were, you had an elevated panoramic view of the sparkling sea below. This wonderful outdoor environment was the focus of my attachment and activities.

The indoor environment was to be quite another matter.

We walked along a dirt track from the station to my new home, known as The Golf House. New Zealanders were crazy about golf and every little village and community had their own golf club. In Pukerua Bay, the club was no longer functional. Our home had once been the club house, hence its name. The flat paddock of land above and behind the house had been its very rough little golf course, or putting range. They'd just shoo away the grazing sheep when they wanted to use it. A little way down the hill, below the house, were some tennis courts, presumably also once part of the general sports club.

## New Zealand bound - March 1956

The house looked very small standing alone on the hillside. Once inside, I quickly realized that I had taken for granted certain modern conveniences. Here, I would experience a new, more primitive way of life, and it was an eye-opener for me. Without much infrastructure to hook up to, the house was a fairly self-sufficient unit. There were outdoor water tanks positioned to collect rainwater coming off the roof, and the toilet consisted of an outhouse and a bucket, which we took turns emptying. The bathtub was a feature of the kitchen. We did have electricity from a central network, and it powered our lights, radio, and refrigerator, or meat safe as it was called. This was a box attached to the outside of the house, cooled by a system of water circulation within its walls. Cooled was the operative word, because nothing kept in there was ever actually cold, unless of course it was wintertime when indoors there was the constant smell of burning kerosene from our heaters. There were two bedrooms. Richard and I shared one, Stan, Carole and Elisabeth, the other. There was a lounge combined with a dining area, an acre of land attached to the little house, and that was it.

That first week, Richard sat me on the handlebars of his bike and rode all around the area, showing me the sites and introducing me to who's who and what's where. Fortunately, I was allowed free range of the wonderful natural surroundings, because home life turned out to be something that had to be endured.

## Settling in

Stan and Richard left the house early every morning for the train to Wellington, but not together. They set out each morning about an hour apart. At the end of the day, Richard would return home from school at about five o'clock and Stan returned from work at about six, when we'd sit down to dinner. Stan was not very involved in life at home. That left Carole to rule the roost, and rule she did. Back in London during the war she had been a sergeant in a female anti-aircraft artillery unit, and she had the medals of distinction to prove it. She excelled at being a tyrant, and she ran the home as if she was still a military officer, with Richard and I her wayward privates. "Don't speak unless you're spoken to," was one of her favorite orders, while most of her utterances to Richard and me were along the lines of "Do this... do that…" Life was regimented, full of rules and schedules. We each had our tasks to do at particular hours on particular days, and they had to be done to Carole's satisfaction – a requirement that seemed to be unachievable.

Several days a week, it was my turn to do dishes. The dirty dishes would be stacked on one side of the sink. I'd wash them and stack the clean ones on the other side. Carole would come along, and after a quick glance at my stack of clean dishes, she'd give me a fierce look and put the whole stack on the other side of the sink to be done again. Never saying a word, I would simply wash all the dishes again, stacking them on the other side of the sink. Along came Carole, who picked up the stack, and put them on other side to be washed yet again, saying to me in her commanding officer tones, "you'll wash them again until you do it properly." If I dared to contradict her (a thing which Richard and I rarely had the courage to do) or even had a look on my face as if I objected to anything she did or said, she would grab my ear and twist it. Or, if she wanted to point out some soil I'd left on the floor, she'd twist my ear and pull my head

## New Zealand bound - March 1956

down to the floor at the same time, shouting at me, "Look what you've done here." On many occasions the exercise brought me to my knees. It was an oft repeated painful experience, although the physical pain was probably outdone by the emotional pain.

What amazed me was the extent to which she was an entirely different person when she spoke to Elisabeth, or when Stan was home. Stan was not entirely oblivious to her military persona. He remarked to me, more than once, that it was better to be married to a block of ice than to a nymphomaniac. I suppose that was how he came to terms with his first wife's infidelity. And what with Elisabeth sharing a bedroom with him and Carole until she was seven, I imagine there wasn't much physical expression of love between them.

Carole was never one to offer a kind word, or an expression of praise or support. Richard and I became accustomed to her habitual barking of orders or making belittling remarks. In sharp contrast, seeing the way she pampered her daughter, felt like salt vigorously rubbed into open wounds. Christmas was a case in point.

"Come on Elisabeth," Carole would say in her sugar-sweet tones, "come and have a look at your presents." Elisabeth would happily dive into her mountain of gifts as Richard and I looked on. We regularly had by comparison a very meager show of one or two Christmas parcels at best. The holiday became more a trial than a celebration, with gifts being a clear illustration of our second-class status.

Richard seemed to be more affected by Carole's treatment than I was. Perhaps it was because he'd borne it longer, or perhaps it was just that we were so very different. I always felt how different I was from both Stan and Richard. My brother was generally miserable and suffered bouts of depression. As it did for me, the outdoors served him as a comforting refuge. When particularly upset, he'd be out of the house and running up the hill where he'd sit and cry until his emotions were spent.

One evening, Carole plunked Richard's dinner down in front of him. He took one look at it, pushed the plate away in disgust and said, "I'm not eating this rubbish." Carole, eyes flashing with anger, replied, "You'll sit there and eat it until you finish it." I looked over at his plate and saw that the meat was crawling with maggots. In a flash Richard was out of his chair, slammed the back door and went running up to the top of the hill to sit under his favorite tree and sob out his misery. I saw, and yet we never spoke of it. We never commiserated or complained to our father. Life was just like that and all you could do was get on with it.

New Zealand bound - March 1956

## The great outdoors

Outside the house, I immersed myself in the welcoming arms of Mother Nature, with whom I got along extremely well. The gifts she had to offer were not only a salve for the soul, but became the source of a significantly growing savings account.

I started my first business initiative at age twelve, within weeks of my arrival in New Zealand. Richard and Stan had picked some mushrooms for our dinner, and they picked far more than we could use. I volunteered to sell them by the roadside, which I did quite successfully. So I decided to repeat the experience. There was another boy selling mushrooms, and I positioned myself a little ways up the road from him. By the time a passing car saw his sign and stopped, they ended up right in front of me. But later, they'd stop alongside me by choice. The other boy had a bad habit of putting pebbles in the bottom of his bags and mushrooms on top, while I developed a reputation as the kid you could trust to have nothing but mushrooms in his ready prepared bags. Finding the mushrooms and knowing which ones to pick was not a problem. These were horse mushrooms, very big and very white, with a beautiful distinctive smell. You couldn't mistake them.

Seeing the money I was earning, Richard offered me a deal. Shy and retiring by nature, Richard was not one to put himself forward and engage in such activities as roadside selling. Instead, he suggested that he would pick the mushrooms, I'd sell them, and we'd share the takings. That suited me fine. Lasting about six weeks during April and May, New Zealand's autumn, the mushroom season was short, but profitable. Carole came with me to the post office and helped me open my own savings account, which kids were allowed to do back then in New Zealand, and whatever you earned as a minor was tax free. That bank account was soon to see a lot of activity, because once the mushroom season was over, I set my sights on possums.

The possum population had grown alarmingly. The country was overrun with them and they were doing a lot of damage, so the government offered two shillings and six pence for every possum killed. The way it worked, a £1 check would arrive in the mail in return for every 8 possum pellets, or tokens as they called them, sent in. My dad earned £5 a week working for the Internal Revenue Department, so a £1 check was significant. My twelve-year-old entrepreneurial sense understood this to be a lucrative opportunity. It also tweaked my sense of adventure.

Out behind the house, I dug a hole and covered it with branches. I checked the next morning and saw that something had fallen in, but whatever it was had managed to crawl out again. My hidden pit was breached, but empty. I dug a little deeper and once again concealed it with branches. The next morning I was excited to see that not only had something fallen in, but it was still there. I could see movement inside. Peering into the hole, instead of the sleek furry body of a possum, what I saw was something rounder and spiky. I had caught a hedgehog. Rather disappointed, I nudged it out of the hole and watched it run away. Okay, I thought, if the possums are going to be wily, we'll have to bring out the big guns. I borrowed a proper trap from a neighbour the same day, placed it in the hole with a bit of flour and aniseed oil as advised, and covered it over with branches again. The next morning there was no need to check the pit. I could hear the screams of the possum, its leg gripped by the teeth of the trap. I gulped, picked up a hammer and left the house to do the dirty deed. Having never encountered a live possum before, no less killed one, I approached the pit with some trepidation, but I was determined to do what had to be done. Heart pounding, I looked into the hole to appraise my victim. The possum looked back and showed me its teeth, obviously capable of doing no small damage. It squirmed violently to

## New Zealand bound - March 1956

free itself, only causing itself more pain and screeching louder. Instinctively, I grabbed its tail as that was the farthest thing from its teeth, and lifted its hindquarters in the air. Then I hit it over the head with my hammer. The first blow only made it angry. It took several tries until I understood the amount of force required for a lethal blow, and finally the thing, if not my pounding heart, was still.

"Oh my good heavens," Carole exclaimed as I stood just outside the back door of the kitchen, one long possum dangling from my raised hand. I wouldn't dare enter the house with it and risk dirtying the floor. "Stan, come and look at this," she shouted. I wasn't sure whether she was impressed or was about to scold me. In the three years Richard had been in New Zealand, and Stan a bit longer than that, neither of them had ever caught or killed a possum. It was an event for the family album. Carole brought out the camera. "Come here Elisabeth, sweetheart. I want to take your picture. Go and stand next to Mike and his possum." Posing Elisabeth next to me holding my prize, she snapped our picture.

Catching and killing the possum was only the first stage toward receiving my monetary reward. Now the possum had to be skinned according to precise requirements. I had to have a pellet consisting of two ears continuous with a seven-inch strip down the back. That accomplished, the skin had to be stretched and nailed to a board, furry side down, to dry out. I poured kerosene over the skin to keep the flies off. After two or three days, providing the weather was warm and sunny, I'd pry the nails out and my possum pellet was dry, stiff and ready for sending. I soon collected my first eight skins, or tokens, and sent them in. A short time later my £1 check arrived in the mail.

That was the start of an occupation I engaged in for the next three and a half years, earning me quite a tidy sum of money.

## Lost & Found

I reinvested my earnings to buy more traps until I had about 30 of them, which I'd lay far and wide. I asked permission of the farmers in the area to place traps on their land and they were only too pleased to oblige. I got into a routine of getting up at dawn and bicycling to the area I was working. I'd climb through the bush, retrieve and kill my night's catch, reset the traps, and get back home with my prizes, five to eight possums a night, in time to wash up, have breakfast and go off to school. Sometimes, as I'd come down the hill, I'd see Richard and my dad going off to start their day's work, and here I'd already earned a pound. There were times I received £5 checks in the mail, and once I bagged 20 possums in one night.

Seeing the kind of income I was receiving from my labours, Stan thought, if this kid can do it, I should be doing it too. He received authorization to work a section of land, got hold of traps, and obtained a license to use a dangerous poison, potassium cyanide, which I, as a minor, wasn't allowed to use. He and Richard set out to lay the traps. They returned many hours later, looking disheveled and exhausted. They discovered the amount of ground that had to be covered, the climbing, digging, and trekking involved. It was too much like hard work for them, and they abandoned the project. Stan let me take over his area. Unbeknownst to him, I did use the poison at least once or twice. It saved me having to use the hammer. As I got older, my possum catching became more sophisticated. I got myself an air rifle. Doing my rounds in the morning, I'd shoot into the trees where I knew the possums would be nesting and sleeping. I became quite the hunter. The money I was to accumulate gave me a feeling of independence, and the freedom to make my own decisions with confidence in my ability to finance them.

I was 16. Early one morning, making my way into the bush, checking and resetting my traps, I detected two furtive figures following me. The next day, about half my traps were gone.

New Zealand bound - March 1956

I was prepared to pit myself against the challenges of nature, but had no interest in fighting thieves. My savings account was healthy and my teenage interests were turning elsewhere. My possum hunting days had come to an abrupt end.

## New Zealand schooldays

Balancing out the oppressive atmosphere within our home, not only was the big outdoors a wonderful consolation, but school was a far happier experience than it had ever been in Birmingham. About one-third of the local school's student body of 30 children were young émigrés from the UK, a fact which gave Pukerua Bay its nickname, POME's Paradise, POME standing for Prisoners of Mother England. The school consisted of two classrooms. The lower class was for five- to eight-year-olds. The higher class, with 15 pupils aged eight to eleven, covered the 3rd to 6th grades. Our teacher, Miss Turner, was kind, clear and patient. I thought she was wonderful. She would divide her time among the age groups and grade levels, each group getting on with their independent assignments while her attention was elsewhere. I'd listen as she taught the younger grades. It was a review for me of things that sounded familiar, but only now became clear. Now I understood and absorbed, and I caught up where before I had been behind. With only five of us in my grade-level group, it was the closest thing to one-on-one instruction. At Pukerua Bay Primary School things came right for me.

A day's outing with Miss Turner was a highlight from Pukerua Bay schooldays. We boarded the train for Plimmerton, about 5 miles away, disembarked and walked back along the coast. We stopped for lunch at some shallow pools inhabited by giant crayfish, commonly known as packhorses. The girls sedately sat on the sand unwrapping their sandwiches, while the boys gathered round the pools, excitedly pulling out giant crayfish and putting them into sacks to take home. I proudly presented my two huge crayfish that evening to my father. He was less impressed than I'd anticipated and made me bury one of them because it was more than we could eat.

After the corrective school experience of that first year, I graduated to Mana College for 13- to 16-year-olds. I now joined the family commuters, except that I travelled alone. Richard had by this time finished school and was beginning his working career as an engineering apprentice. He and Stan now travelled together back and forth to Wellington. I was on a different schedule and got off two stops earlier.

Each morning Carole prepared sandwiches for everyone to take with them for lunch – two sandwiches, each neatly sliced in half. When Elisabeth was old enough to start school, she was treated to a delightful variety of fillings. Even Richard had some variety of lunchtime fare. I, on the other hand, was given peanut butter sandwiches every single day. I hated peanut butter, and that's why it was all I ever got. Carole had noticed one day that I brought back two uneaten sandwich halves and on inquiring, discovered my culinary quirk, which was not to be abided. I was told that from that day forward I would have nothing but peanut butter sandwiches to the end of my days. It took me a while to discover that there were children who actually liked the thick brown stuff, so sometimes I got to trade my sandwich for another kid's meat pie or some such thing. To avoid Carole's wrath, I would throw my leftover sandwiches out the window of the train on the way home.

Years later, I told the story to my little son Paul who thought it was the funniest thing he'd ever heard. He blurted out one day, "Granny, do you know that dad used to throw his peanut butter sandwiches out the window of the train?!" There was an

## New Zealand bound - March 1956

awkward moment of silence during which Paul wondered why no one laughed. Nor was there any hint of the wrath such a discovery might have unleashed from Carole when I was a child under her care and control. Now, as two adults, the passage of time had afforded us a different perspective. In fact, it might have been from that moment on that Carole and I began to get on together. We learned to like one another, unlike my brother Richard. He never got over his childhood hatred of Carole, to the extent that after Stan's funeral, Richard remarked "Now we don't have to have anything to do with that bitch anymore," and he didn't.

In contrast to the welcoming atmosphere of Pukerua Bay School, Mana College was a "wipe that smile off your face" kind of place. The teachers were mostly former WW2 officers who demanded a military level of obedience. It was very strict, and caning was a frequent occurrence. We had school uniforms, including caps, and were expected to be dressed properly at all times. One morning, I got on the train without wearing my cap. Unfortunately for me, there was a teacher on the train who had seen me embark, capless. The train arrived at our stop. We both got off and walked to the bus. He said to me in a cold, impersonal and slightly threatening voice, "Carlson, see me in my office." Right then I knew it was not going to be a good day.

I obediently went straight to his office on arrival at school. He was waiting for me, cane in hand – a very large cane.

"Carlson, you were not wearing your cap. Bend down."

Now it just so happened there had been an incident at school that week when a rather large Maori student, one Bully Rene, upon being caned across his bare lower back, grabbed the teacher in a head lock and slammed his head against the wall. Emboldened by the new feeling of rebellion in the school, I replied, "I'm not bending down."

The teacher could hardly believe my arrogance, and became wild with fury. He started slashing the air with the cane, making a fearsome whoosh, whoosh sound. Well impressed with the intensity of his passion, I thought I'd better comply or there could be worse to come. I bent over.

He gave me four lashes with all the strength he could muster. I did not enjoy it. Later, back in class, sitting somewhat uncomfortably, our class teacher said, "Hands up whoever hasn't done their homework."

So many hands went up around the room that everyone started laughing. The teacher, on the other hand, found no humor in the situation. The entire class was punished. The girls all lined up in the hall to receive their detention or whatever mild punishment was their due, while the boys queued up in a long line outside the teacher's office to receive their caning. When it was my turn, the class teacher, who had obviously spoken with my first cane master of the day, said to me, "It's been a bad day for you Carlson." I thought I detected the smallest glimmer of a smirk, evidence that he did find some things humorous after all. And with that he delivered my second caning of the day. In one year at Mana College I received 44 lashes of the cane, each one duly registered by a notch on my belt.

I was not very happy there, to say the least. The situation worsened until coming to a head at the start of my third year. It was during one of the weekly army cadet training sessions in which all students of 13 to 16 were required to participate. We were riding along the beach in the back of an open vehicle. Our task was to jump out while it was in motion. Each boy ejected himself in turn, rolling on the sand as he landed, and then it was my turn.

## New Zealand bound - March 1956

The teacher shouted at me "Jump Carlson," and I froze. Not wanting to interrupt the smooth rhythm of jumping boys, he pushed me out of the vehicle. I fell badly and hurt my arm. I realized something was seriously wrong as it was very painful and I soon lost all feeling in my hand. The training session closed with a parade during which we were meant to be holding our rifles. My arm hurt too badly, and I couldn't hold it properly. The teacher looked at me and said, "Hold your rifle."

"I can't, sir," I answered. He shouted at me, to no avail. I could not comply even if I'd wanted to.

At home that evening, I told my father what had happened. He examined my arm and put it in a splint, and the next morning he took me to the hospital. I was diagnosed with a broken arm, which had to be set and put in a cast. Next, Stan went to the headmaster to lodge an official complaint. The teacher who pushed me was brought to task, but it did me no good whatsoever. From then on he marked me, looking for any excuse to deliver a reprimand or punishment. He finally caught me on some minor complaint, got me into his office and gave me a hell of a hiding – six of the best, as he fondly called it.

Again, I reported back to my father and announced that I'd like to transfer schools. I thought I might do better going to Wellington Technical College where I'd learn a trade. The next day there was another confrontation between my father and the headmaster, but this time I was pleased that Stan simply informed him, "My son is leaving your school."

So it was that during the first few weeks of my third year at Mana College, I happily transferred to Wellington Tech, which after Mana, was not only a definite improvement, it was a delight. One of the first schools that encouraged freedom of expression and held the student and his welfare as all important,

Wellington Tech also did an excellent job of preparing students for a practical trade. There were courses in construction, engineering, electricity, plumbing and so on. I decided to study electricity, which has remained a lifelong interest. At age fifteen, 1959 proved to be a happy year. I enjoyed the studies, the teachers, my friends, and it all seemed to be over far too soon. 1960 was the year when things started to go wrong.

# Disenchanted

I had really enjoyed my first four years in New Zealand, living in Pukerua Bay. I could tolerate home life because I had another active and satisfying life outside. But things happened in 1960 that changed everything. That was the year the family moved from Pukerua Bay to Porirua East, and I lost my escape route.

Moving to Porirua was a step up, even though the house was state-owned, with subsidized rent. It was closer to Wellington, and it was bigger. But the surroundings were far more urban. There was no bush-covered hill to run up as you crashed out the back door. No golden beach down below with places to swim or shallows for fishing. No forest to hunt in or just to lose yourself. Without my outdoor escape route, home life began to close in on me.

It all came to a head in one angry moment that served as my catalyst to leave. Stan and Richard were trying to put together a new bed we'd acquired. They weren't doing very well, and tempers flared. I watched for a while and then offered my opinion as to what they should be doing. That was apparently the last straw for Stan and he threw the spanner at me. It just missed my head. I took that as an excuse to get the hell out. Without saying a word, I grabbed my small leather suitcase, packed my things, which didn't amount to much, and left for Pukerua Bay. I arrived

## New Zealand bound - March 1956

at the home of my best friend, Rickey Branson, and asked if I could live with them. They were very nice about taking me in. I shared Rickey's room, which fortunately had an extra bed in it. I made no contact with my family, but I suppose they put two and two together and figured out where I was. After living there for a week, I received a phone call from Stan. He told me to return home immediately, which I did. When I arrived, nothing was said. There were no lectures. In fact, they seemed to be embarrassed about the whole incident. It was never talked about, and we maintained an uneasy truce from then on.

Coinciding with the move, 1960 was also the year I started working. I ceased to be a schoolboy, a carefree child, and at age 16 became a member of the workforce. Stan had arranged a position for me as an electrician's apprentice. This meant I was bonded to work for him for the next five years. It started off well enough, but the thought that this drudgery was all there was to life for years ahead, became more than I cared to contemplate. I also realised I had to get out of Porirua. It was driving me insane – the family life, and the new suburban environment which I never liked and never would. I wanted out.

I decided my best option was to travel. After having stuck with my apprenticeship for a year and a half, I approached my father and told him I wanted to go back to the UK to see my mother. I'm afraid I used her as an excuse. What I really wanted to do was get the hell out of there, get on a ship and have a ball. Life had a terribly unsettled feeling about it, with no sense of belonging to a family unit, nor any satisfaction from it, and that was also something I wanted to get away from.

Since I would be leaving for England, Stan got me released from my apprenticeship with the understanding that I'd continue it in the UK. I'm not sure whose understanding that was – it wasn't mine. I left my apprenticeship and looked for a well-paid job so that I could earn my passage. I got a job making clay pipes with Humes Pipeworks, which was offering a lot of money for that time. In fact, I was earning as much as Stan. With a salary of about £22 a week, £5 going towards my keep, I managed to save £220 for a one way fare, and another £200 for spending.

I was still living at home, but my release valve was weekends. Every Friday to Sunday night I'd be in Pukerua Bay where there was a lively social life. From the age of 16 to 18, life included cars, alcohol and girls, and a loss of innocence with summer beach parties that started in the evening and lasted into the wee hours. I'd stay at my friend Rickey's most of the time, and sometimes at a girlfriend's. I was happiest away from home.

# V
# Back to Birmingham - August 1962 - March 1964

## The voyage

Stan arranged my passage, and I telegraphed my Mum to say I would be coming. She telegraphed back to say that she and Rod would be there to meet me on my arrival.

The day of my escape arrived. I boarded the Johan Van Oldenvanevelt in August of 1962 with high expectations, no thought of consequences and not a single formulated plan as to what I'd do once back in the UK. The only understanding I had with myself beyond getting away and having a ball on the ship, was that this would be a visit, and I'd eventually be back in New Zealand.

The JVO, as it was called, was Dutch manufactured and the largest diesel ocean-going vessel of its time. It operated as an immigrant ship bringing settlers to New Zealand and taking on New Zealanders, or Kiwis as New Zealanders affectionately refer to themselves, who were eager to see the world. Stan was at the dock to see me off along with a couple of my mates, Rickey, Joey Barns and his wife, and my girlfriend at the time, Karen. Early marriages were common back then, which was another good reason to move on.

Knowing it was already a done deal, Stan nonetheless said he would let me go only on condition that I promised I would not drink. I made the promise, only to break it on the first night out. The promise to myself to get away and have fun had a far stronger pull. My accommodation was a dormitory cabin shared with 25 other young men. I was among the youngest but determined to drink along with the best of them, which I did at the Get Acquainted party. There were quite a few single young women on board as well. I got to know a few of them, and took a few on off-shore dates.

That first night out we travelled from Wellington to Auckland, and from there on to the Fiji Islands, docking at Suva, the capital. I leaned over the rail for a view of the Fiji Police Brass Band that marched out to meet the ship, adding fanfare to our arrival. Little did I know that some years down the road the island would be my home for a time and I'd have business dealings with the Fiji Police Force.

Next stop, Tahiti, where a cabin mate and I hired a couple of Vespas and set out to explore the island. We loitered around the set of *Mutiny on the Bounty*, but never got to see Marlon Brando. We were drenched in a tropical storm, dried and fed by a kind local family, and ended the day in a nightclub frequented mainly by locals. Drinking our beers, we were entertained with native dancing, which got us wondering if the beer was very strong or if we were actually seeing hips and bums gyrate at that incredible speed. Eventually approached by two pretty Tahitian teenage girls, the four of us left the nightclub for another venue and a friendly chat – and we'll leave it at that.

A word about my cabin mates. All young men between the ages of 19 to 28, they hailed from New Zealand, Norway, Holland, Ireland, and England. Nearly all of them were émigrés to New Zealand, returning home for one reason or another. Harry was

## Back to Birmingham – August 1962 - March 1964

English, like me. He was 21 and returning to the UK with the aim of finding a wife and bringing her back with him to New Zealand, which he did. The friendship we struck up on the ship was to last a lifetime.

The odd one out was Lars, who told a sad tale of witnessing his parents, who had been Nazi collaborators, being tortured and killed by Norwegian partisans. One day during the voyage, he asked if he could borrow my sandals. A while later, on deck with my friend Harry, we saw Lars standing on the ship's railing wearing a life jacket over his clothes and my sandals. He suddenly leapt from the railing into the sea. We looked on in shock as he began swimming in the direction of a small island, and realized no one else had noticed. We had to tell someone, fast. Grabbing a ship telephone, we announced to the bridge, "Do you realize a man has just jumped overboard?"

All hell broke loose as the ship reversed its props, sirens and hooters went off and big lifebuoys with flashing lights flew over the side. Thrust into reverse, the ship shuddered so violently with the strain, it felt like its rivets would pop. The crew lowered a small craft over the side, with the ship's doctor and a few sailors, who rowed out to the oblivious swimmer. Lars had to be subdued before they got him onto the boat and he spent the rest of the trip in the ship's hospital under psychiatric care. The only casualty of the day was my sandals. They were lost at sea.

Having traversed the Pacific, our next stop was the Port of Callao serving Lima, Peru, where I heeded some advice and toured the capital with a local Spanish newspaper tucked under my arm so as not to be a targeted tourist. After that, we headed toward the Panama Canal, threading our way through the locks in the opposite direction, giving me a replay of the experience I'd so enjoyed six years earlier.

## Lost & Found

We were scheduled to carry on toward Cuba, but the region was in the throes of the Cuban Missile Crisis, so we detoured toward Florida and docked at Fort Lauderdale instead. Getting a ride down to Miami, I was witness to the heavy air traffic coming in a steady stream from Cuba, carrying escapees from Castro's regime.

One more stop along the east coast of the US gave me a taste of the Big Apple, gliding past the Statue of Liberty, enjoying the view from the Empire State Building with my date of the day, and wandering the city streets.

The Atlantic crossing on the last stretch of our journey brought us to briefly dock in Lisbon, Portugal and then finally, we made our way to Southampton where my partying and play time would come to an end, and I'd have to come to grips once again with the ordinary everyday realities of life. Once it deposited its UK bound passengers, the ship carried on to its final destination in Amsterdam, thus completing what was to be among its last voyages. Not long after, in December 1963, the JVO (by that time sold by the Dutch to the Greeks and renamed Lakonia) caught fire with the loss of 128 lives, and sunk off the coast of Gibraltar as it was being towed to port.

Back to Birmingham – August 1962 - March 1964

## The party's over

My Mum and Rod were waiting to greet me at the dock in Southampton. I was a sorry sight as I disembarked. The previous night's good-bye party had lasted till morning and left me the worse for wear. I was slightly hung over, noticeably lacking a clean shave, and carrying my dirty clothes tied in a bundle, having sold my suitcase for some extra cash. Rose and Rod last saw me as a smooth-cheeked 11-year-old. I can only guess what went through their minds at the sight of me now. Initial greetings accomplished, Rod asked if I had any money. I answered no, and he gave me a 10 shilling note. I don't suppose my mother was overly impressed with me at that moment. A little while later she took me to task about the £40 she had wired me per my shipboard request and demanded I pay it back. Rose and Rod had driven down from Birmingham to meet me, and now the three of us piled into the car for their second three-hour drive of the day.

We arrived home in Birmingham, and there I was, back in my old room. As if time had stood still, it looked exactly as it had when I'd left. Well, the same but not the same. The difference was me. From my new height, the proportions were different, as were my perspectives in every way. I was now 17, with a world of new interests on the horizon. And my half-sister, Susan, was different too. No longer the little girl I remembered, she was now a gangly 13-year-old, and she seemed rather indifferent to her big brother, a young man she no longer knew. Once I reestablished my relationship with my surroundings, I was able to appreciate the home life with Rose and Rod. It was good. It was comfortable. Compared to living with Stan and Carole, home life in Birmingham felt far more caring.

So now that I was back, what was I to do with myself? I had formulated no plan beyond getting on that ship and having a bloody good time. Now I would begin getting acquainted with consequences. I knew I'd work in the UK, and having watched the barmen on board ship and the fun they seemed to be having, it looked to me like a dream job. As the closest thing to it, I found employment as a waiter at the Plough and Harrow Hotel, which was quite an up-market establishment. (In hindsight, I feel certain that my biological father, Robin Jacobs, had worked there, but I couldn't prove it.)

I quite enjoyed working as a waiter, until I got my first pay check. That's when I collided head on with harsh reality. As opposed to the last job I had in New Zealand where I was earning a very good salary, here I would be bringing in no more than £4 a week. I suddenly felt trapped. I realized it could take me years to earn my passage back. At least I had that much of a plan – I'd always intended to go back.

Looking for advancement, I left that hotel after a time and got a job at the New Inn Hotel where I did a course in hotel management. After completing the course, I was offered a job as a Trainee Assistant Manager at the White Swan in Central Birmingham. By this time I had been living with Rose and Rod for 14 months. I now moved into the White Swan Hotel and lived there for the remainder of my time in Birmingham, which turned out to be another six months.

Back to Birmingham – August 1962 - March 1964

## The life of a Birmingham bachelor

Shortly after arriving, I reconnected with some old classmates, but the person who was to be my closest friend during this period was a fellow called Henry. A friend of the family, he and I were the same age. He was working part time for Rod in a takeaway chicken rotisserie chain that Rod was managing for his sister's wealthy son, Patrick. Henry and I clicked right away and discovered we had very similar interests – girls and beer!

Rose and Rod agreed to let me take over the attic, which I turned into a bachelor's den. I installed a music system, dimmer lights, and made it the perfect venue for privacy, romance and whatever. Henry and I took it in turns; one night it was his, the next night it was mine. Once, approaching the 'whatever' stage, Rod caught me coming downstairs toward my bedroom with Marsha, my pink-haired date, in my arms – I made a rapid retreat back up to the attic.

Henry informed me one day that he'd happened upon a treasure trove of lovely young women. Known as the Nurses Home, it was an orphanage for abandoned young children, mostly under the age of five, adjacent to a children's hospital. Providing a place of work for nurses in training, it was also a school for aspiring nurses and included a dormitory that one could only enter with a password. Not that that kept me out. As I recall, the password was "gossamer" at the time. Henry had gone out with one of the nurses and asked if I'd like him to arrange a blind date for me. That's how I met my first wife.

We made it a double date, Henry and Sharon, April and me. We picked the girls up at the nurses' school, went to the park, and then to an outdoor beer garden. I would describe what she looked like, or what I liked about her, if I could conjure up a clear image. It seems my emotions and my memories are closely linked. Because she was subsequently deleted from my life, early memories of her seem to have been erased. In any event, the date went well and we continued seeing each other. As our relationship progressed, I made it clear that my intention was to return to New Zealand and set up home there. April was considering it.

April met Rose and Rod and we went on holiday with them to Cornwall, with everyone getting along amiably. However, as happens in young relationships, we had a serious quarrel, following which I made my decision and booked passage to return to New Zealand, with or without her. As my departure loomed imminent, it was April's parents who took the initiative to effect a reconciliation. April called to say her parents wanted to see us both together. They would be treating us to tea and snacks at Lyons Tea shop in central Birmingham, a very popular venue. Never one to turn down a free lunch, I went along. And so it happened that we were reconciled, with April promising to join me in New Zealand as soon as she'd put some money aside. With a little help from her family, particularly a wealthy Aunt, this turned out to be quite soon indeed, a mere four months later.

The night before my departure, we had a small goodbye party. April was there, and Henry, and a few other friends. Everyone was feeling sad, except for me. I was realizing my plans, doing my thing, with nobody's help. It felt good.

The next morning was cold and cloudy, reflecting Rose and Rod's somber mood as they drove me to Birmingham Airport. I, on the other hand, was quite excited – I was off again – and so very pleased to be out of there. Although home life was kind and comfortable, I didn't feel a sense of belonging. Birmingham was dreary. New Zealand was in my bones and I missed it. Parting from my mother at this stage in life felt quite different than when I had last parted from her at age 11. I believe she was far more upset this time than I was.

## Back to Birmingham – August 1962 - March 1964

Adding to the excitement of my departure was the fact that this was the first time I'd be boarding a plane and flying. The twice weekly service between London and New Zealand had begun just under a year earlier in April of 1963, and I'd be flying on the latest model of the world's first passenger jet, the BOAC de Havilland Comet 4. But first I had to get to London. Flying in a piston-engine aircraft on the initial leg of the journey helped me appreciate the comparatively smooth, quiet flight of the jet. I was quite taken with the experience, which influenced my decision years later to learn to fly myself.

I had ample opportunity to experience landings and take-offs on that first flight. The route took me from Birmingham to London, on to Rome, then a stop in a Middle Eastern country – and all I remember about that was that it was not Israel – from there to India, then Indonesia, Darwin, Sydney, Auckland, and then, after a long wait between flights, finally on to Wellington. All in all it was about 37 hours of travel time. As long as that may seem today, it was still a lot quicker than a sea voyage. The new jet service changed the lives of New Zealanders, reducing their feeling of isolation and increasing exponentially the numbers of Kiwis going abroad to see the big wide world.

# VI
# Going home to New Zealand - March 1964

The sun was just setting as I completed the last leg of my journey, the flight from Auckland to Wellington. I was able to make out the shape and landmarks of the city before it got dark, and it was a lovely feeling to be home again, in the arms of New Zealand's spectacular Mother Nature.

I had sent a letter to Stan and Carole telling them of my planned return and giving them the details of my arrival, but received no response. Nonetheless, as I walked out into the arrivals hall of Wellington International Airport, there were Stan and Richard, waiting to greet me. As usual, there were no displays of affection, but it was a friendly reunion. Neither my Dad nor Richard had ever boarded a plane. I was performing another family first in flying halfway across the globe, again setting me apart as an aberrant member of the family. I felt that they were a little bit in awe and perhaps a bit apprehensive, mixed with the excitement of their first time at the airport to meet a passenger.

Feeling somehow empty-handed upon our greeting, I felt I ought to have had some message or gift to convey to them, to Richard from his mother, to Stan from his ex and mother of his children. I distinctly felt from Rose that she would have liked me to tell Richard that his mother loved him and to give him a small token of that fact, and to tell Stan that he was remembered, perhaps even missed with some regret mixed in. But she had overtly

## Going home to New Zealand – March 1964

conveyed to me neither sentiment nor token, so this I could not deliver. Instead of carrying greetings, I offered woeful stories of my impressions of England, especially Birmingham, as the pits of the world. I expressed my need to find employment at the earliest opportunity, as I had one pound to my name, and to get on with my life. As we left the airport, Richard returned to the boarding house where he lived and Stan drove me to the family home in Porirua.

On our way home, I told Stan about my appendicitis attack. Following a first occurrence on board ship, I had experienced a recurrence in Birmingham resulting in my hospitalization and appendectomy. I mentioned to Stan that I had felt terribly lonely there, with precious few visits while I was in hospital. My father's response was, "Well, you're among friends now." I think that was the closest I ever got to a welcome home hug.

It was late at night when we finally arrived, but Carole and Elisabeth were waiting up to greet me. The formalities completed, considering I had just been travelling for 37 hours, I was soon in bed and asleep.

The very next day, I got myself a job at my previous place of employment, Humes Pipeworks. However, my Dad was not entirely pleased with this, and I worked there for only two days before I gave in to his pressure. He disapproved of the friendships I had previously developed there and worried that I would return to bad habits and undesirable relationships. When he discovered I had visited a former friend's estranged wife a couple of nights later, his worries were confirmed. Actually, I didn't mind turning over a new leaf instead of going back to where I had been, so I found myself a job at a hotel in Wellington, which I had to admit was work with more of a future to it than that offered at Humes Pipeworks, even if the starting pay was lower. The St. George Hotel, where I worked for about five months, proved to be a fortuitous choice. It afforded me an eye-witness experience of exciting events.

In 1964 the Beatles came to New Zealand. They flew into Wellington, and were brought straight to the St. George Hotel. With police barriers holding back screaming crowds of young girls, the famous foursome entered the hotel and were shown to their rooms. I overheard Ringo Starr ask where his room was. "You're in it, sir," the bellboy replied, to which Ringo said, "This is like a fucking wardrobe to me." They ordered a couple of crates of cola and two bottles of Bacardi rum, and were not seen again until the evening, when it was time for them to depart for their performance venue. The elevator door opened to reveal four very drunk young men. Paul McCartney leapt out of the elevator and gave a sweeping bow to the delighted applause of onlookers.

For the duration of their stay, no one was allowed in or out of the hotel, including hotel staff. We were all on watch to keep the crowds away, as young girls were all but scaling the walls and climbing the fire escapes to try to reach their idols. I indulged myself in a naughty diversion when I stood by one of their windows and waved to the crowds as if I was one of the Beatles. I was greeted by appreciative screams. The hotel manager, less impressed with the rock stars, remarked that if he hadn't known who they were he would be loath to allow them into his hotel. Although disdainful of his famous guests, he did quite well from their visit. Following their departure, he had their sheets torn into little squares and sold for no small profit.

About a month after the excitement of the Beatles' visit, April, my UK girlfriend of several months, arrived in New Zealand interrupting a brief romance between myself and a young Australian pantry maid – a pretty good indication of just how committed I was to embarking on a lifetime relationship. April

## Going home to New Zealand – March 1964

was welcomed into the family home and stayed with us briefly – in a separate room of course; conjugal living before marriage was not acceptable back then. She was resident there just a few weeks, but long enough for Carole, commander of the home, to start complaining about April's hair clogging the bathroom drain. April rented a room at the YWCA, and shortly after, started working at Hannah's, a Jewish-owned shoemaker shop in Wellington.

No sooner had April arrived in New Zealand, than her mother began cooking up a plan to get her daughter back home with her prospective new husband. Enlisting the help of her very wealthy daughter-in-law, April's mother presented us with her idea of a rescue plan. If we returned to the UK, she would purchase a small English pub/hotel which would be ours to run, manage, and do with as we liked. It was a tempting and generous offer and I believe April thought so, but there was no way I would consider it even for a moment. I wanted to be in New Zealand, end of story. Aside from that, I'd always been too self-reliant, filled with my own initiatives and ideas about how to run my life, to take kindly to anyone's offer to "set me up".

About three weeks after April moved out of Stan and Carole's, I changed jobs and moved out as well, but my new address was rather more up-market than the YWCA.

I began work at the Wellington Club, where I took up residence. It was established in 1841 as a gentleman's club with accommodation for such VIPs as visiting politicians and the governor general, the queen's representative in New Zealand. Now, the Wellington Club served as an exclusive venue for members of the wealthy upper class in the area. Of course, the staff quarters were nothing like the opulent guest accommodations. All the glitz was out front for the members. Staff quarters were mixed, with shared facilities, all very basic.

Even so, it was quite a nice address.

The club included an exclusive restaurant where I started out working as a waiter. Although a "men only" establishment, wives could dine there as guests of their husbands. I was later promoted from waiting tables to managing the bar. During the year and a half that I worked there, I served an illustrious clientele, from New Zealand's Governor General, Brigadier Sir Bernard Ferguson and Brigadier Gilbert, Head of New Zealand's Security Intelligence Service (SIS), to then Prime Minister, Sir Keith Holyoake. I was privy to many an interesting conversation regarding politically hot issues of the time, and as barman I catered to the less public side of club members. I recall one member in particular, formerly New Zealand's UN ambassador, for whom I opened the bar early every morning to serve a breakfast of three double gins.

Rather inevitably, April and I began to plan our wedding. We chose a nice Wellington suburb church for the event and a date in November, New Zealand's spring. While making our wedding plans, April and I saw a newspaper ad about homes being built in Levin, a town just north of Wellington. It sounded attractive, so we looked into it. We were advised to apply to the government for a State Advances Loan. To supplement that, we took out a second mortgage through an insurance company, and we saved like crazy, successfully managing to scrape together enough for the deposit.

The wedding was a modest affair, with neither my mother nor April's family in attendance since air fares were prohibitively expensive. My New Zealand family were all there, Stan, Carole and Elisabeth – Richard was out of the country – and a few friends, as well as my boss from the Wellington Club.

Arriving back from our honeymoon in South Island, we got off the train and entered our new home. We were starting married life with a 3-bedroom house of our own on a quarter of an acre of land. I thought that was not bad at all for a just-married lad of 22.

## Acclimating to adulthood

Although April had trained in the UK to be a nurse, she had not yet qualified. For that she would need further training. She opted instead for jobs that didn't involve working shifts, while I held a wide assortment of jobs, taking advantage of any opportunity that presented itself. My hotel management training would find no outlet here; there was nothing in the area worth calling a hotel. Willing to try anything, I worked in a wallpaper factory and on a car seat production line, as a field hand picking apples and as a gardener on a wealthy family's estate. The most consistent and satisfying work I did during this period, sometimes as a volunteer and sometimes as a paid employee, was with institutionalized adults deemed unable to manage independent living. It certainly developed my social consciousness. I felt I was doing something meaningful and worthwhile, and contributing to the community. I was helping unfortunate folk, and in so doing I felt a useful human being.

Against the background of my varied work life, home life was transforming itself as well. Within two years of marriage, our two boys were born, Paul and Alex.

We moved several times in the next few years. April gave up work and became a full-time Mum, as was the norm back then, while I assumed the breadwinner role, which kept me less involved in the day-to-day upbringing of the boys, again, a norm of the times. When they were babies I didn't change nappies or feed them, but once they were old enough to toddle about, I was more hands on. I loved playing with my boys, and I was proud of my family. Life was good. For the first time in my life, I was experiencing true blood relationships – Paul and Alex were mine, of me and like me, like no one else in my family had ever been.

After Alex was born, I felt a need to do something more with my life. I needed something that would inspire me. I needed to find something different, purposeful, or at least consistent. That was what motivated us to downgrade our residence and move to Wellington for studies. We rented our house in Levin and moved into a caravan, one notch below a trailer home. This stretched our income while I went back to school catching up on things I should have learned in college, taking the exams to qualify as an instrument pilot, and even taking a course in chaplaincy in a psychiatric hospital.

In Wellington, of all places, I first rubbed shoulders with Judaism. I worked as a deliveryman for Stan Hirsh, delivering pies fresh from the bakery in early morning calls to small owner-operated cafes and workers' breakfast joints. The most popular pie was egg and bacon, still a firm favorite in New Zealand today.

Bacon pies notwithstanding, Lenny Kravitz was my first Jewish acquaintance and I was constantly asking him questions about his practices, his holidays and his beliefs. He always took the trouble to give me full explanations in what was to be my earliest encounter and growing interest in Israel and the Jewish People. When he celebrated his son's bar mitzvah, he invited me to the event, which I attended with a friend of mine. It turned out to be a strangely unforgettable experience.

The rabbi suddenly approached me, took both my hands in his, looked for some time into my eyes and said "Shalom". My friend, who received only a perfunctory but polite hello, was killing himself laughing and said to me afterward, "Mike, he thinks you're one of them." Did he see something no one else saw? Was it a premonition…? Like an unexpected ripple in time, it was shades of things to come.

My desire to go back to school and my queries about Judaism were all part of a serious time in my life. Here I was, 24, married and father of two, and I was drifting from job to job. I needed to look for a new beginning. I was experiencing a kind of spiritual awakening. It had nothing to do with one religion or another. It was more a deep personal faith. I simply became a believer.

We later sold the Levin home and moved from Wellington to Auckland, following a job opportunity in social work and rehabilitation. We rented a place for a time and eventually built our own home in Torbay on the North Shore of Auckland where we settled in, the boys started school, and I took up flying.

## Learning to fly

A friend of mine was learning to fly.

"Mike," he said, "why don't you come too? We'll take you up with us – you, me and the instructor."

Okay, I thought, sounds like fun. I arrived at the airport early and told one of the instructors I was waiting for my friend who invited me to join him during his lesson. The instructor said, "Why don't you get your own license?" and promptly took me for a trial flight. It was exhilarating. I loved it. And that was that. I was bitten by the bug. For the next ten years, I flew two or three times a week.

The year was 1972, and I was lucky to be learning to fly before what became known in New Zealand as the "oil shock", that is, before the price of oil skyrocketed. My qualification flights cost me $9 an hour. Today it would be more like $60 or $70 an hour. I soon acquired the requisite forty flight hours and received a New Zealand pilot's license, which included being able to land on grass and hilltops, as well as an Australian license that included a written exam and an outback flying exercise.

There were three types of licenses reflecting varying levels of pilot qualification. Having achieved the most basic, I next went straight for the highest level, the license that gave free range to fly when and where you liked, in almost any conditions, anywhere in the world. That was the one for me. I became one of the few highly qualified pilots in the country.

I had big plans. A friend and I purchased a plane together, with the intention of flying around the world – nothing less! According to our plan, which I talked about to anyone who would listen, we would circle the globe in six to eight weeks.

## Going home to New Zealand – March 1964

With our sights set high, we bought a Cherokee Arrow, which looked a lot like a Spitfire. This was a particularly fast plane, and there were precious few around like it. In fact, global travel aside, it was a very good choice. This unique aircraft became our golden goose. We made a lot of money with that plane, renting it out to the aero-club on Auckland's North Shore. Aside from its thrill factor, it was used for training and qualifying pilots for high-speed aircraft. In fact, my buddy and I had to qualify before we could take possession of it.

We flew to Christchurch to pick it up. Once there, we went up with an instructor, and soon each of us had our qualification. The plane was now ours. We boarded our very own aircraft for our maiden voyage back to Auckland. We were like two school kids just out for the summer holidays, high-fiving and euphoric. In hindsight, I might add we were just a little cocky.

The wind was strong that day, and not being all that experienced as pilots, it seems we underestimated its strength. We were well aware of the military base we would be passing and its restricted airspace creating a significant no-fly zone, and had thought we were sufficiently clear of it. The wind, however, pushed us closer than we intended to go. We suddenly became aware of a military jet, which appeared close alongside us to accompany us down to the military landing field. We were asked to identify ourselves and were given orders to make a sharp right into the military zone and land.

I definitely did not want to do that. It was my understanding that we had only touched the outer edges of the military air space. We'd identified ourselves, I reasoned, and were clearly neither a hostile aircraft nor did we present any threat. I boldly refused the order and held my course for Auckland. The jet eventually abandoned us and headed back to base. As we touched down in Auckland's airport, our radio barked out an order to report to the control tower. The civil aviation authorities, all ex-military, were outraged. We had to appear before a military hearing, which to my great relief agreed that since we'd been positively identified, it was unnecessary to bring us into the military zone to land. We were let off with a warning, and so ended the saga of the maiden flight in our very own, unique little speed demon of a plane.

For our round-the-world trip, we needed to carry more fuel than the plane's tanks could hold. We got permission to remove the back seats so that we could put an extra gas tank inside. Then the story of a US pilot, who had done something similar, hit the news. He was flying with an extra gas tank inside the plane, which blew up rather spectacularly when the pilot lit a cigarette. From then on carrying a gas tank inside the plane was outlawed. It would now be impossible to fly our plane around the world, putting an end to our Phileas Fogg ambitions.

Going home to New Zealand – March 1964

## **Fear of flying**

I wanted to instill in my boys my own love of being airborne. Unfortunately, I believe I set the stage for their current fear of flying. Shortly after receiving my basic pilot's license, I offered to fly April's parents, together with April and the boys, to South Island for a visit to this beautifully scenic area. In addition to lakes, fjords and glaciers, it was known for its majestic mountains – the very ones featured in *The Lord of the Rings* films, including the country's tallest, Mount Cook. What I hadn't taken into account was that I had been used to flying over fairly flat land and had absolutely no experience flying over mountainous terrain. (Nowadays training in mountain flying is a prerequisite for receiving a PPL, the basic license.) Well, flying is flying, I thought. How difficult could it be?

We set out, all of us quite happy. Then, just to complicate matters, we flew into heavy clouds over South Island – another feature not part of my training or experience. I managed to climb through a hole in the cloud cover, and as we emerged into clear skies an unforgettable sight, dead ahead, filled our windows. Mt. Cook loomed up rather ominously, much closer than one would wish to see it from a plane, and we were headed straight for it. My blood ran cold and I'm not sure if there were gasps, or if everyone just held their breath. Desperately implementing defensive maneuvers, I flew through a mountain pass so narrow I thought I could feel the wing tips scraping the sides. By the time I landed at the nearest small landing strip in Tekapo, I emerged from the plane in a cold sweat, breathing heavily. My passengers were in not much better state. I called control and cancelled my flight through the mountains to Queenstown. To everyone's credit, we got back into the plane and flew to Christchurch instead – a nice flat area. But the seed had been planted. To this day, both Paul and Alex have to down a few stiff drinks before they board a plane.

But considering the amount of time I spent in the skies, mishaps were rare. There were in fact only two, both involving malfunctioning landing gear, with no serious consequences. I used the plane for work, and eventually became comfortable flying through mountainous terrain as well. In 1973, four of us, two couples, flew to Queenstown to spend a few days there. We fell in love with the place and decided that one day we'd move there.

## Finding my place in the work world

Three years after moving into our Torbay home, we sold it and moved to Whangarei, New Zealand's northernmost city. Whangarei was away from the hustle and bustle of the big city, which for us was attractive. Secondly, there were job opportunities there, and thirdly, Auckland had experienced a property boom and the value of our home had risen nearly threefold in three years. The move to Whangarei proved fortuitous. It was there I found my career niche.

I hadn't been particularly happy with the long string of odd jobs I had held. In Whangarei, once again looking for a job, a friend suggested I check the option of selling shares for the Southern Cross Building and Banking Society, which offered savings and mortgage schemes. I decided to give it a shot.

On my first day out, I knocked on a few doors, received threatening growls from a few dogs, polite declines from potential customers and made no sales. As I drove away from my last attempt of the day feeling that this was a no go, I recognized my doctor walking along the road. I stopped and offered him a ride. Making polite conversation, he asked what I'd been doing. I launched into my explanation of what it was all about. When I'd finished, he said, "I'd like to buy some shares." That sudden and unexpected success turned me around and I thought, hey, this is a good job! I can be independent and work my own hours, and there's no ceiling on my income other than the amount of energy I'm prepared to invest. That suited me fine, harking back to my possum hunting days. Bitten by the bug then and there, I set about my work with enthusiasm, and considerable success.

## Moving up toward a downward slide

The year 1976/7 turned out to be momentous. That was the year my buddy and I sold our Cherokee Arrow after nearly three glorious years. We had bought it for $18,000 in 1974, and sold it in 1976 for $24,000, having enjoyed a nice income along the way from its hire. I had grown quite fond of my aircraft, and when we sold it, it was a sad day indeed. The decision was entirely a matter of economics. I needed the money to finance our planned family trip and 4-month stay in the UK. At the same time, we were building a home in Queenstown on a rather large block of land I had purchased. We returned from abroad in October '76, and by January '77 we were ready to make the move to Queenstown with the completion of our new home. As it turned out, we didn't share it for very long.

The move to South Island brought with it a different lifestyle. Queenstown was a party town, and party we did. It was also known as the home of short marriages, and I suppose we helped promote that statistic as well. It didn't take long before we made new friends and were integrated into the town's social scene, or should I say entangled. We became involved with other people, both of us having numerous flings. In 1977, my life took a major slide, involving an excess of sex and alcohol. Strangely, the start of this downturn coincided, almost to the day, with the death (unbeknownst to me then) of my biological father. It makes me ponder the fundamentalist belief that if an evil spirit inhabits a person, upon that person's death it moves on to the next of kin.

Our involvement with other partners did nothing to improve our marital relationship. During a conversation with her doctor, when April unburdened herself regarding our unhappy state of affairs, the doctor asked her, "Have you considered divorce?" She hadn't until then. Now she gave it serious thought. It became an option we discussed. Then it became a heat of the moment thing and she moved out with the boys. It was stupid really, because we still had feelings for each other. When the dust settled, we should have said we're silly buggers and reunited. We had attempted reconciliation at one time or another, but we never seemed to be in the same mind at the same time. In the end it was just too hard to unravel. I finally said, "To hell with it, how much do you want?" and goodbye. In hindsight it all seems a bit ridiculous. Nonetheless, by 1979 we had reached an amicable agreement. April wanted to return to the UK with the boys. We agreed that they would spend school holidays with me, meaning either that I would travel to the UK to be with them, or I would pay for their airfare and bring them to New Zealand. At the ages of 11 and 12, Alex and Paul seemed destined to echo something of my own childhood, only in reverse.

Going home to New Zealand – March 1964

## The second time around

The only part of my life that hadn't changed by the move to Queenstown was my job. I continued selling Building Society shares, working from home, and knocking on doors, choosing my targets based on where the money was – businesses and farms. Although I no longer owned my own plane, I flew even more now on business, using hired planes. It was a very convenient form of travel, especially now that I was living in a more isolated area. A bachelor once more, I rented out the family home thinking I might live there again one day, and lived modestly in a rented flat or in motor camps when I was travelling. I threw myself into my work.

In 1980, I was travelling through the mountains around Queenstown, this time by car, stopping at farms along the way and aiming to end up in Wanaka. My plan, whenever arriving at a new town, was to visit its accountants and lawyers. The Building Society I worked for had an excellent manager who had prepared a sales manual and training sessions that I'd attend in Auckland. But I also developed my own strategies – overcome resistance before it arises, and know where it will be coming from. A problem I encountered was that I was selling North Island shares in South Island, in competition with the South Island Building Society. My strategy therefore, was first to visit a town's bank and present myself and the benefits of my proposals to the manager. Once he was on my side, the job would be easier.

On February 2nd, I strode into the Wanaka bank, asked to see the manager and gave him my presentation. When I'd finished he said to me, "to be honest with you, I don't need any of these shares, but would you like to speak with the staff?"

He set me up in the staff room with coffee and sent the staff members in, one at a time. Among the staff members, including a few young females, was 19-year-old Rochelle. By the end of my presentation I'm not sure who was more taken with whom. She bought ten shares, and I was not prepared to say "thank you and so long."

"I'd like to spend my commission on you," I told her, "Would you like to come out with me and go for a flight?" Why not go whole hog and impress her, I thought. She declined my invitation but did agreed to go for a meal the next night, a Friday, on condition that I came to her house to meet her mother. That I did, meeting also a number of her many siblings. Rochelle was smart, cheerful, and an altogether most attractive young woman. For her, I was someone new and exciting on her small town horizon. Barely two months after having met, we were engaged.

To celebrate the engagement, we planned a romantic weekend in Makaroa. Not too far from Wanaka, it was the kind of place tourists call "out in the wilderness", but for us, it was just another lovely area of South Island. Rochelle's mom made us a rum pot – a liqueur to pour over ice-cream. We were pleasantly settled into our room with candles, wine and soft music, when surprisingly, there was a knock on the door. The hotel manager peered in and said, "Oh, I hope I'm not disturbing," to which I replied, "Well, actually you are." Not to be put off, he asked if we'd like to book a jet boat ride the next day. Wanting to get rid of him as quickly as possible, I thanked him and said we'd think about it. Getting back into the mood of candles, wine, soft music and my lovely Rochelle, within a few minutes there was another knock on the door. I couldn't quite believe it. I went to the door and there was the hotel manager once again. "We're only two people short of a full booking. If you don't book now, you'll miss out." I realized I'd have no peace until this guy had filled his boat. We did enjoy the boat ride the next day, and

## Going home to New Zealand – March 1964

more to the point, we enjoyed the rest of our evening without interruption.

In June, Rochelle came with me to England to meet my boys, my parents, and visit with her sister Pamela and husband Danny, who lived in London. It was Rochelle's first trip abroad. In fact, it was her first time off South Island.

I wanted to show her the sights and on our second day in London we dressed up, looking very smart, and went off to Buckingham Palace to do what tourists do. We stood behind the wrought iron gates peering in at the palace and telling ourselves that a glimpse of the queen was surely imminent. Excitement rose among the palace gazers when a member of the palace staff emerged and walked toward the gates, surveying the crowd as he approached. He looked right at Rochelle and me, walked over to the policeman on duty, pointed at us and told him to open the gates and let us in. Had we been selected for an audience with the queen? Should we have prepared something to say? Amazed at our good fortune and wondering where we were going and what was about to happen, we followed the gentleman into the palace. We hadn't known, but now and again tourists were invited in to sign the visitor's book, which we did, feeling very honoured indeed. When we emerged and rejoined the tourists behind the gates, we were met with stares and whispers. "Who are they?" people wondered. It was a wonderful beginning to our visit, and we felt rather special

While in London, we decided to do a family tree together – Rochelle researching my family, and me hers. We went to Somerset House and began our research, but to Rochelle's dismay, she was thwarted right at the beginning – she couldn't find my birth records. She found birth records for Rose, Stan, Richard… but no Michael Carlson. I thought she must be doing something wrong. I tried showing her how it should be done, and sure enough, I also came up with nothing. We asked for help from a staff member who expressed some exasperation at having to show us what to do, only to discover that no records were to be found for the birth of a Michael Carlson. She said to me, "You know people can find out nowadays if they've been adopted."

Hang on, I thought, what's this?! We went out for a beer. I phoned Rose and said, "Mum, Rochelle is with me. Guess where we are… We're at Somerset House where they keep all the records of births and deaths and marriages. We're doing each other's family tree and I can't find my birth records. Was I born during an air raid?" I knew Richard had been. "Richard was born on Healthfield Road. Where was I born?"

"Same," she answered.

All her answers to my questions were so reassuring that I didn't bother going back to Somerset House. Later, when Rochelle stayed in London with her sister and I went to Cornwall to see Rose and Rod, and their daughter Susan and her husband, I asked Rose again where my long-form birth certificate was. That was when they told me the story of the V2 rocket landing on Somerset House. Luckily, it hadn't exploded, but Somerset House notified other areas not to send any records until after the war. The reasoning was, I was born after that rocket attack and that's why we couldn't find my birth certificate. The issue was laid to rest and I put it out of my mind.

That summer Rochelle met my boys, Paul and Alex. During their school holiday the four of us toured England together and had a great time. We rented places to stay here and there, and spent some time staying with Rose and Rod in Cornwall. It was a thoroughly successful introduction, both of Rochelle to the boys and of the boys to their dad in his new partnership.

## Going home to New Zealand – March 1964

When we returned from the UK, Rochelle's mom invited us to stay with her. I had my own room, and we were "good children" under her mother's roof. We then moved to the house in Queenstown as soon as I managed to get the tenants out.

On January 2nd 1982, two years after we had met, Rochelle and I were married. We set up the Queenstown home as a B&B run by Rochelle, who also worked in a hotel washing dishes and waitressing. We worked like the dickens and saved every penny we could, in order to embark on our planned building projects. We eventually managed to build three terraced flats on our block of land, plowing all the income from the B&B into the flats. We finished the first two in two years, and rented them out. We added to our mortgage to continue our development and then paid everything off with a bonus from the insurance company that we worked for. We ended up with four properties to sell and values were rising.

Lost & Found

## New work ventures

The following spring I was headhunted by an insurance company. It sounded like a good offer, and I felt it might be time for a change. I left the building society and started selling insurance instead of savings plans. By the second year I was ranked top salesman, countrywide. Rochelle and I worked together. I was the front man, out selling, and Rochelle did all the paperwork in our home office.

I was contacted by an international brokerage company claiming they had a good position for me in Fiji, just three months a year. It involved my becoming a broker who worked for a client, rather than for an insurance company. Fiji was very attractive for tax purposes. It was also very much warmer than the cold Queenstown winters. In fact, Rochelle and I had holidayed there and liked it so much we had bought a holiday home. So spending three months a year in Fiji was a pleasant prospect, as well as convenient for us, and we took up the offer. Ralph Grant, the General Manager of the insurance company I was working at, was not happy about it, but as I was a valuable salesperson, he learned to live with it. Rochelle and I also frustrated him by consistently turning down the tempting loans Ralph was throwing our way.

My annual bonus one year came to $60,000, exactly the sum we owed on our property. We decided it would be a good idea to use it to pay off our mortgage. Despite our differences, I had become quite friendly with my boss, Ralph Grant, and he and his wife came to stay with us over Christmas. There we were, suffused with the holiday spirit and relaxed in the Jacuzzi together, sipping wine and soaking up the bubbly warmth, when I made the mistake of broaching the subject of my bonus.

"Ralph," I said, "how's this? You can keep my bonus and use it

## Going home to New Zealand – March 1964

for paying off my mortgage."

"Now why would you want to do that, Mike? You've got great terms on your mortgage and you deserve your cash bonus."

"Well, that's what I'd like to do," I answered.

The climate changed instantly. Ralph didn't like that. I discovered that our friendship went only as deep as my benefit to the company. The insurance company liked to own its employees. Their policy was to keep employees in debt to them and encourage the debt to grow with their highly tempting loan offers, recallable at the company's pleasure. Some of my colleagues were living way beyond their means, and I wondered what would happen to them when payment was demanded on their loans.

The day I was to receive my bonus came and went. As I had been awkward, the company now decided to delay it, perhaps indefinitely. Not one to take kindly to being owned, I called a meeting of all the sales staff and easily convinced them to back my cause, for their sakes as well as mine. I phoned Ralph there and then, and told him we were prepared to walk out en mass if my bonus was not released to me in the next 24 hours. The next day, $60,000 turned up in my bank account. I paid off my mortgage and left the company. We decided to go for Fiji full time.

My boys, Paul and Alex, had returned to New Zealand to live with us some years before, each of them returning as soon as they reached the age of 15, when they were allowed to make their own decisions. By the time we were preparing to make the move to Fiji, the boys were old enough to live on their own and they stayed on in Queenstown. Eventually their mom returned to New Zealand as well.

## Life in Fiji

We started out in Fiji selling life insurance to ex-pats from New Zealand, Australia, and the UK, but our first few years were not very promising. It was slim pickings indeed. We had to draw on our savings and eventually sold our holiday home and rented a place, just to have enough money to keep going. The timing of the sale was fortuitous. We got a very good price, just before the market dropped dramatically due to the military takeover.

Finally, after working too hard, too long, for too little return, there was a breakthrough. The South Pacific Bureau for Economic Cooperation was a UN vehicle of about 120 members, and they had just lost their medical insurance. They rang us up and asked if we could help. My immediate reply was, "Yes, of course." My second reply was, "I'll get back to you soon." I hadn't dealt with medical insurance until then, but decided now was the time to start. I flew out to Hong Kong, the best and nearest place for generating business schemes, and spent over two months putting together an insurance package I could sell. Having organized my own product, I returned to Fiji fully equipped to meet their needs, and ours.

While living in Fiji, I often felt ashamed to be white when I saw how the native Fijians were treated. For instance, no Fijian was able to obtain insurance due to a policy of no insurance to blacks, for fear they wouldn't be able to meet their payments. Rochelle and I were among the few whites who were friendly with the locals. Following the 1987 coup d'état, most whites left Fiji. We, however, continued to be on good terms with the indigenous population and were accepted as pro-Fijian. In fact, a local news article featured a photo of me and the leader of the Fijian military coup shaking hands. Rochelle was quite friendly with his wife who was a teacher.

## Going home to New Zealand – March 1964

Now our fortunes really changed. We provided medical insurance to the entire Fijian military establishment and police force. We also developed a group insurance package which we sold to tribes. It was a win-win situation where both we and our clients benefited. The medical insurance I provided was cheaper than any obtainable in New Zealand, and it included air fare to New Zealand for treatment.

We lived and prospered in Fiji for a total of eight years. When Rochelle became pregnant, we decided it was time to head back to more stable surroundings. We wanted the baby to be born in New Zealand, and in fact arrived back in Queenstown just three weeks before the arrival our daughter, Miriam.

I had forgotten how much I enjoyed parenthood, and Rochelle certainly enjoyed it. When Miriam was four years old, we took a hiatus from the work world. We lived on a boat on Doubtless Sound, surrounded by some of the world's most beautiful scenery and living off nature, fishing and eating our catch. Once Miriam saw a pod of dolphins and excitedly called out to them. The dolphins, babies among them, seemed to recognize her child's voice. They swam over to us, rolling in and out of the water, and accompanied our boat for some time, much to Miriam's squealing delight. That was how we spent some four months together – betwixt sea and sky, among nature's creatures and beauty, living sublime simplicity. It was a wonderful, happy time.

Since we had returned from Fiji to a very different environment, we had done with selling insurance. But never ones to stay idle, Rochelle and I set up a little tourism business, which we ran for the first four years after our return. We brought our boat up to commercial standards and took tourists out on Queenstown's Lake Wakatipu, sightseeing and fishing.

## The rest of my life in a nutshell

Preferring a rural to an urban existence, we eventually moved to our fixed up batch on the small island off the coast of Auckland. Miriam went to school there until the age of 12, when she went off to boarding school in Auckland as there were no schooling options for children over 12 on the island. From an early age, she became a very independent young lady. She eventually finished school and went on to Auckland University to become an engineer. Paul returned to the UK, living in London and working as a fund manager at the Royal Brompton Hospital, and Alex became a very successful finance controller in Auckland. Meanwhile, Rochelle and I entered the world of real estate. We did a crash course in Auckland and became licensed agents, just to delve into something new, take on a new challenge, and enjoy some profit from it too.

After a scare due to Rochelle's illness, treatment and subsequent recovery, we thought a totally new project was in order to clear our heads of health problems. We focused our search on Tuscany, Italy, where we'd once holidayed and like most visitors, fell in love with it. Another consideration was to have someplace we could escape to and avoid the difficult cold winters on the Island. We bought a two-storey home just inside the ancient walls of a tiny mountaintop village, and put a lot of work into fixing it up. The village's permanent population of 35 reside in homes with carved stone lintels over their doorways bearing their dates of construction. The two opposite us read 1640 and 1729. I removed our home's external plaster to reveal the beauty of the building's original stonework. With new window frames, double glazing and two working fireplaces, it's cozy even in winter. We were very pleased with the results, as our many guests have been.

The plan was to spend six months in Italy and six months in New Zealand… until a third option appeared on the horizon.

# VII
# Search and discovery

It was a calm summer's day in February 2008, just as Rochelle was about to leave the island for Auckland, that the thunderbolt struck and my life took an unexpected turn.

Richard's letter, replete with adoption documentation, arrived like a spear to the heart. My head in a turmoil and my whole body reeling with the shock of it, I managed to get Rochelle off to the airport and accomplish my day's chores. Finally back home that evening, alone with my thoughts and feelings of betrayal, my very identity called into question, my first reaction was to launch into a frenzy of phone calls.

I wanted the truth and nothing would deter me from pursuing it. I promised my three children I would find their true grandparents. I was about to embark on an information gathering campaign that would consume the major part of my life, my time, and my thoughts for several years to come.

First, I verified the documents received from Richard by viewing online the registration of birth of one John Robin Howard – apparently, that was me. To eradicate any further possible doubt, there was the identifying number. The Adoption Order Richard sent, displaying both my former and current names, cited the same number as that appearing on the birth certificate of John Robin Howard. It appeared again as the entry number on the Adoption Certificate, and appeared anonymously and without explanation at the bottom of the only birth certificate I had ever had until then – the short form birth certificate of Michael Carlson, which indicated only my name, gender, and date and country of birth. Looking at it now, the document spoke its message to me loud and clear. Any identification of parentage was conspicuously absent.

The next morning, my first thought was that I wanted to know about Birmingham during the war years. I wanted to speak with someone who had been there. I immediately thought of Joe Walton, who lived on the island. He was about seven years my senior and had lived in Handsworth, the area of Birmingham where I grew up. How likely was that, to find such a person on a small island, population 450, in the southern hemisphere? I felt G-d's hand must be in it. I called Joe and he was soon sitting opposite me describing life in Birmingham during the war. Two hours later I had a pretty good picture of the chaos the war wrought on relationships, with husbands away fighting, and lonely, frightened women meeting similarly lonely and frightened soldiers, while everything was tenuous and uncertain.

Continuing my campaign of phone calls, I phoned my adoptive mother's brother to confront him with my newly acquired knowledge and learn from him whatever he could tell me. Having safeguarded the family secret of my adoption all these years, he was not about to encourage my search. He said I was the natural son of an American GI stationed in England during the war, and that I would never find him.

I phoned Richard, the deliverer of my life-changing news. As I'd always thought of him as my big brother, the one person in this world with whom I shared childhood experiences and who was in my corner, I suppose I was looking for some comfort or support from him. Richard answered the phone from his home in Perth, and the first thing I said was, "Richard, what's going on?"

## Search and discovery

It was clear that he had no idea of the extent to which I was completely thrown off balance. It seemed that no one did. Even Rochelle and the kids seemed to react with, oh well, it's just one of those things. Never mind. Get over it and move on; it's just one of life's hic-ups. But to me, not knowing who your parents are felt like a great deal more than a hic-up.

"I knew you would take it well," Richard offered, but provided no further information than what he'd already put into the letter.

"How long have you known?" I asked him.

"I'm not going to go into that," Richard replied.

"Well why didn't you tell me when you were here a year ago?" I asked.

He mumbled something about thinking it not important saying, "what difference should it make to you now?" I couldn't possibly have explained the very huge difference it made to me. The conversation became rather emotionally charged and Richard, recalling a photograph of Rose holding me up as a baby, said, "I think they loved you more than me." What hidden resentments lurk within human relationships.

I phoned Elisabeth, my New Zealand half-sister, or so I had thought. "When did you find the papers?" I asked her. After my adoptive father, Stan, had died in 1982, his wife, Carole, had remarried, and I knew that when she passed away in 1988 all her personal belongings were packed into a box and sent to her daughter, Elisabeth, in Melbourne. Elisabeth claimed that only late last year, in 2007, she had decided to go through the box and came across the documents. Perhaps she had been advised of its having been a family secret and gave Richard the responsibility, sending the documents to him.

Elisabeth did however admit to hearing a slip from our Aunt Anna, Stan's sister. "Aunt Anna once blurted out that you were adopted." And then she said something that later made the penny drop. "You should have put your hand up for some of that money," she said, referring to Aunt Anna's inheritance.

Next I called Susan in Birmingham, Rose and Rod's daughter. "Guess what. I just found out I'm adopted," I told her. She didn't believe it. She was shocked. She had known nothing about it.

But it still puzzled me. Why had Richard suddenly decided to tell me now? And then remembering Elisabeth's words, it finally dawned on me – money. Richard and his wife Gillian had gone to live in Perth, near our elderly Aunt Anna. When Aunt Anna passed away, I spoke with Richard saying I wanted to send flowers. "No," he said to me, "don't send flowers. No need. Don't do anything like that."

"You should have put your hand up for some of that money," Elisabeth's words echoed in my head. Richard and Gillian were the sole recipients of Aunt Anna's fortune. Elisabeth was the sole recipient of Stan and Carole's inheritance. I think Richard wanted to rule me out from making any claims on his mother's legacy, and in fact, once Richard and Gillian ascertained that there was no fortune to inherit, they cut off all contact with Rose, as well as with her daughter, Susan.

In one of our last conversations I said to Richard, "I thought you were supposed to be my brother," with all the emotional baggage that went with the word "brother". It was a major point of upset and disappointment for me. I thought, in all the world, at least I'd had a brother. My last words to Richard and Elisabeth were, "I'll leave you two gold-diggers to your own devices." Closing the door on my family that was not, I redoubled my search for the family that would be.

## Search and discovery

My entire being now focused on discovering my true parentage. First thing to be tackled was my own identity. Richard's documents had given me names. I could finally obtain a proper birth certificate. A myriad of things were coursing through my brain, things that could be looked at anew and reinterpreted. I now understood why my mother, that is, my adoptive mother, had only ever presented me with a short form birth certificate. Her having lied to me about it was another matter that echoed deep in my gut. This was the first of many things that would now be understood in a new light.

Although the discovery of my birth origins was clear cut, receiving documentation was not. Upon requesting a copy of my original birth certificate, which apparently was in the hands of the courts, I discovered that the authorities would not release it unless it went through an adoption support agency such as NORCAP. I paid my fee and became a member. Similarly, my application to the Birmingham City Council for adoption records was met by an impervious wall – they could not, or would not, be of any assistance. With the help of NORCAP and dogged persistence on my part, including my application to the Birmingham Magistrates Court, I finally did receive my original birth certificate and, quite some time later, the full adoption report.

## Looking for my mother

Having verified who I was, it was time to embark on discovering who my parents were. The second precious piece of information culled from Richard's documents was the name of my birth mother, and now that I'd seen the official online birth registry, I had her maiden name as well. Claudia Faye Howard, formerly Gates. The name beckoned to me from the page, like a tiny chink in the door to my past that could be grabbed and pried open. That was the piece in the puzzle that served as a pointer, directing the path of my search. And so my second request to the General Register Office included everything I could get my hands on regarding this presumably married woman who failed to include a father's name on her child's birth certificate.

I found five birth listings of women named Claudia Faye Gates and I requested and paid for birth certificates for all of them. I also found a marriage document of a Gates to a Howard, which I ordered as well. With some trepidation, I searched for a death certificate, hoping I wouldn't find one.

The documents arrived, and Rochelle and I examined them with care. Comparing dates and ages, we managed to identify the relevant Claudia Faye Gates. I now knew that my mother had been not quite 22 when I was born. She had married at age 18 to one Keith Broderick Howard, age 20. By March 2008, one month after learning of my adoption, having found no death certificate for Claudia Faye Gates or Howard, nor any current UK address registered to that name, I cautiously concluded that my birth mother had either emigrated, or had remarried, changed her name and was still alive and resident in the UK.

I now enlisted the help of AAA-NORCAP, the special department for Adults Affected by Adoption. Their service included liaising between the parties – the parent and child –

## Search and discovery

preparing them for the emotionally charged meeting. However, they did not involve themselves in the actual tracking down and locating of a parent. For that, they referred me to the NHS, whose policy was strange indeed. It seemed they were of two minds as to how much information they should give out in helping one to initially find the other. Loath to offer me any direct information, they suggested I could ask them leading questions to which they could provide yes or no answers. This resulted in our playing a game of 20 questions.

I started with the question: had she remarried? Yes, they replied. Is she living in London? Yes, they replied again. Back to my research, what I eventually turned up was a divorce document between a Nick and Claudia Faye Allen, but I found no further documentation for any Claudia Faye Allen. Back to the agency. Had she remarried again? Yes, they replied. After a great deal of prodding and cajoling, they offered the information that she now had an Italian-sounding name. With that piece of information, my searches turned up a Claudia Faye Cavaleri, and with the help of an online site, 192.com, I now had her address in London.

Excited by this breakthrough, I contacted my son Paul who was living in London, and gave him the address. He went round with a camera, hoping to catch a glimpse of her. It was an apartment building with a doorman and reception station, so there was no way of entering anonymously. After hanging around outside the building for a while, during which time no 86-year-
old woman appeared, Paul left and sent me a photograph of the only thing he managed to document, the building she lived in.

I now knew that Claudia Faye Cavaleri, currently 86 years of age, had been married three times and was alive and resident in London. Stage one of my research successfully completed, locating my birth mother, I was anxious to see her, to get acquainted, to see photos of what she looked like when she was the young woman who became my mother, the young woman I might have grown up with, whose face would have been imprinted in my childhood memories. I wondered if I looked like her. And when we met, what would I say? How do you do, I'm your son? Hello Mum? Thank you for seeing me? Why did you abandon me? A terrible mix of emotions was stirred up – excitement tinged with fear, longing dampened by resentment, and beneath it all, a deep hurt and sadness, mourning for what had been lost.

But these feelings were nothing compared to what I would feel after her response to the request for contact mediated by NORCAP.

I returned once more to NORCAP with definitive information as to the current status of my birth mother and her whereabouts. They suggested as the next step that I write a letter and enclose a photo of myself. They would make contact with her and subsequently deliver my letter.

Making their initial contact, a representative of NORCAP wrote to Mrs. Claudia Cavaleri, which prompted her to phone. Afterwards, Marilyn, my NORCAP contact, sent me a copy of their letter and a transcript of the conversation. Based on that, I could imagine the scene:

*Claudia was nursing her second cup of morning tea as she opened her mail.*
*It consisted of the usual bills, adverts and donation requests, except for one that she'd not heard of before – AAA-NORCAP, adoption support agency, Department for Adults Affected by Adoption. Are they looking for donations, she wondered as she opened the letter.*

## Search and discovery

*"Dear Mrs. Cavaleri," it began. "There is someone from New Zealand who wishes to make contact with you, whom you haven't seen for a very long time." What in the world is that about, she wondered. I don't know anyone in New Zealand. "We would be obliged if you would phone our offices at your earliest convenience."*

*How odd, she thought, I'll have to phone and set them straight. It's obviously a mistake. But in the back of her mind, there was a disturbing echo of events long past. The word "adoption" did not sit well with her.*

*She rose from her kitchen table and walked over to the telephone, letter and contact details in hand. She dialed the number, reassuring herself it was simply a mistake. A woman's voice answered.*

*"Hello, is that Marilyn?" Yes, came the reply. "This is Claudia Cavaleri. I got your letter. I'm afraid there must be some mistake. I know no one from New Zealand."*

*"Well, Mrs. Cavaleri, the person who would like to make contact with you has to do with events that took place in Birmingham in 1944."*

*Claudia's breath caught in her throat. Her heart began to beat faster as the name of the organization suddenly took on a sinister significance, and reluctantly her mind put together the words "adoption" and "1944 Birmingham". There was silence on the line while Claudia composed herself, cleared her mind and hardened her heart. She would not have ghosts popping out of the past and coming back to life – into her currently neat and orderly life. Admit one ghost and another might appear, too painful to remember.*

## Lost & Found

*Waiting for a response, Marilyn finally added, "Mrs. Cavaleri, does the name John Robin Howard mean anything to you?"*

*The name was like a spear, involuntarily causing the hairs to rise on Claudia's arms. That name. The name she had chosen – a lifetime ago. She was told he had died. Hadn't she suffered enough then? Did it have to be brought back now, a lifetime later? No, it didn't, she told herself, and it won't. I won't let it. Neither my children nor my grandchild need ever know anything about it.*

*"Mrs. Cavaleri, are you there?"*

*Finally Claudia responded sounding very articulate and calm. "I did the best that I could in a very difficult situation," and after another long pause, "it was the war."*

*"I understand, Mrs. Cavaleri," Marilyn replied. "The person who contacted us would very much like to meet you. We have a letter from him that we'd like to deliver, and photographs. We'd be happy to talk to you about it and help set up a meeting."*

*Maintaining her calm, Claudia replied in her firmest voice, "No. There will be no meeting. I want nothing to do with this. I'm not interested in meeting with him."*

*"Can he at least have a photograph of you?"*

*"Absolutely not."*

*Marilyn continued, kindly and patiently, "You know the law has been changed now to allow biological parents and adoptive children to make contact with each other."*

*Claudia listened calmly and attentively. "Well, I thank you for contacting me Marilyn, but I don't want to hear any more about this matter."*

*And with that, Claudia hung up the receiver. She noticed the letter still clutched in her hand and she tore it, once, twice, into unrecognizable pieces and dropped it in the bin, letting the lid close over any further trace of the letter, of her past. She stood staring at the closed bin for a time, took a deep breath, and pushing all thought of the incident from her mind, she turned away, as she had turned away before, and resumed nursing her second cup of morning tea.*

I received a phone call from Marilyn, on my birthday of all days.

"Mike, I'm sorry about this. There's no easy way of telling you, but I have to say I've contacted your mother and she doesn't want to meet you, she doesn't want to give you a photograph, and I'm very sorry it's come to this, but I'm afraid that's all we can do."

I was devastated, dumbfounded. Not only was I given away as a two-month-old bundle of innocence, but now I was being rejected once again, once and for all. I was simply a bad memory. A dirty secret. A bit of rubbish to be swept under the carpet. Not even to acknowledge my existence, my birthright. To refuse any contact or knowledge of me. Why? How could a mother react so? To her I was less than nothing. My victory over finding her turned into a final defeat. My enthusiasm and excitement at the thought of a future meeting, a coming together, were ruthlessly dashed to bits. My emotions hit an all-time low.

But not for long. I was hurt, but I was also angry. And I talked about it with friends, trying to come to grips with it, to understand. Continuing her supportive contact, Marilyn called again a few days later and apologized for having delivered the news on my birthday. She suggested I write another letter to Claudia, expressing my disappointment at her refusal to meet, which I did and posted directly to Claudia myself.

Slowly, I managed to see it from her side. The shock of it. The desire not to upset her current life. And perhaps more than anything else, the desire not to reopen old wounds, the pain of those years – the war, the love affair, the joy and the shame of the pregnancy, the heartbreak of giving up her first born (or so I thought) for adoption, the divorces, and perhaps no small amount of guilt feelings. It was all best left buried in the past. I tried to come to terms with the fact that attempts to reach my birth mother had hit an impervious wall.

But I knew she had children, and they were my siblings. This, I would not be denied. I tracked them down, flew from New Zealand to England, and knocked on their door. Here's how it happened.

My online research uncovered a Charles Allen, born to Claudia and Nick Allen, and currently an accountant, resident in London. I made an appointment. It was an impressive office, not lavish, but certainly comfortable. I sat, waiting to be invited into the inner sanctum of his office, when a woman approached and introduced herself.

"Mr. Carlson? How do you do? I'm Harriet, Charles's sister. He'll be with you in a moment." I nearly fell over. I had come face to face with my sister! Two siblings in one meeting – that, I hadn't anticipated.

"Would you like something to drink," she asked politely.

"I sure would," I replied, with a stiff whisky in mind. She

## Search and discovery

returned with a cup of coffee.

Finally, I was ushered into Charles' office.

"It's very nice to meet you Mr. Allen," I said, extending my hand. "I've come a long way to see you. In fact I've just flown in from New Zealand."

We had a long discussion about matters of double taxation between the UK and New Zealand. Finally, I decided to lay my cards on the table. I told him of my discovery that I had been adopted and that I was trying to make contact with my mother, which prompted him to ask how he might be of assistance, and finally to ask, "What's the real reason for your being here?"

"We've got the same mother," I told him getting right to the point. He seemed to freeze, receiving the news in silence and passively studying me now with a slightly different gaze.

"You're quite sure," he said finally.

"Absolutely, without a doubt. I can show you my birth certificate to prove it," I answered.

"And why have you waited till now to come forward," he asked, not unreasonably.

"It was only recently that I discovered I was adopted as an infant, and I've been tracking down my true parentage," I replied.
I then offered Charles the relevant documents for him to copy, and he hurried away to do so. Upon his return he grasped my hand and seemed to come very close to hugging me as he gave voice to a new thought, "I have a brother," he said.

Harriet later told me that after I left the office, Charles called out to her, "Harriet, you'd better come with me and have a few drinks. I've just met your brother."

Once they'd absorbed the information, Charles and Harriet agreed to meet with me again. When I'd finished telling them my story, Charles said, "You realize you've got another sister too, from another marriage."

"No," I told him, "I didn't know."

Harriet and Charles were both fathered by Nick Alanis, or Allen, the Anglicised version of the name, and it was from them that I learned that Nick had been Claudia's boss at the restaurant in Birmingham where she worked. After their marriage broke up, Nick returned to his native Cyprus, where he ended his days. My third sibling, Margaret, was fathered by Claudia's third husband, Anthony Cavaleri.

A few days later I met Margaret. Harriet had set up the meeting and joined us to make the introductions. It was quite pleasant, we got along well, and I felt that here were people with whom I could remain in contact.

Having told my newfound siblings, Charles and Harriet, about my abortive attempt to contact our mother, Claudia, through NORCAP, Charles asked, "Would you like to meet your mother?"

"Of course I would," I said with barely disguised eagerness, "but I don't want to upset her."

"I'll see what I can do," he said.

Charles confronted his mother. "I've just met your son," he told her. "We'd like you to meet him, and he'd very much like to meet you."

## Search and discovery

Claudia became extremely upset and would not be budged. She stubbornly refused to have anything to do with any meeting, and beyond that, even forbade her children from giving me or showing me any photographs of her. Perhaps she was afraid I'd recognize her on the street one day and she'd find herself staring into the face of her buried past. I was only to find out some two years later the reasons for her reacting with absolute horror at the prospect of confronting her past.

Margaret, my third new sibling, tried to explain her mother's shock and refusal to face the fact of my existence.

"After the adoption," Margaret told me, "she was apparently pining over the loss of her infant. Your grandmother told Claudia when you were 18 months old that you had died of diphtheria, to get her to finally let go and forget about it."

How much greater the wrench of the separation and the guilt of giving away one's infant might have been had she known I lived, and how much guilt involved in facing me a lifetime later. I was doing my best to temper my disappointment with understanding.

Following my meeting with Harriet, Charles and Margaret, I could now put together a more coherent timeline for my mother. After her divorce from Keith, her first husband, Claudia Faye Howard had entered into two more marriages, the first in 1949 with Nick Alanis, known as Nick Allen, who I now knew had been her boss at the restaurant where she worked. He fathered her second child, Harriet, conceived while Keith was overseas. This apparently taxed Keith's powers of forgiveness beyond their ability and precipitated their divorce. Not quite six and a half years after Claudia and Nick were married, during which time Charles was born, she divorced once again and entered into her third and last marriage with Anthony Cavaleri, who fathered Margaret.

I subsequently met Margaret on another occasion, together with her daughter who proudly shared with me photos of their home in Cornwall, nicely displayed on her tablet. And suddenly, there she was. My mother. I didn't need to be told. I knew at once who she was. I drank in the image with a silent, hello, mother. It did me a lot of good to see that picture. She looked a very nice lady. She was smiling, looking very happy, sitting next to Margaret. I think she had blue eyes, like mine. Rochelle was with me and she said afterwards about the photo, "Mike, that was unmistakably your mother."

Funny, I had a similar experience when I first saw a photo of Robin Jacobs – I just knew he was my father.

I'm going to try and get Margaret's daughter to give me a copy of that photo – my one glimpse of my mother. One tiny thing to actually touch and hold, a single tangible connection with the woman who gave me birth - the woman who meanwhile forbade her adult children from any further contact with me, and like good children, they complied. Sometime later, Harriet renewed contact after her husband had convinced her that turning her back was not right.

Search and discovery

## My paternal legacy

From the meeting in London with my newfound siblings, I flew to our home in Tuscany, Italy. A tiny, remote, mountaintop village, one reaches it after a 20 minute drive up a steep, narrow road that hugs the mountainside as it winds through thick forest. I did a lot of thinking driving up and down that mountain. On the journey down to pick up Rochelle from Rome airport, I told myself I had done what I could to try and reach my mother. I had found her other children, my siblings. There was nothing more I could do. Arriving at a decision, I suddenly said to myself, "your mother's a dead end. Leave it, Mike. Find your father."

I now turned my attention and energies to tackling the mystery of my paternal parent, but where to start? Perhaps Keith, Claudia's husband at the time of my conception, knew the identity of Claudia's illicit partner. It was worth a try.

I spoke to NORCAP and shared my idea that Claudia's first husband might give us a clue. Working together online, we found the death certificate of Keith Broderick Howard. It also showed his age at the time of death, and it all fit in well, verifying we had the right person. The death certificate named Elaine North, Keith's daughter, as informant and it included her address. At this point NORCAP was out of the picture, able to offer no further help. I was on my own.

Keith's daughter lived in Tenbury Wells about an hour and a half drive from Birmingham. I contacted her by post saying I'd like to be in touch with her, as I was investigating my family tree and there could be a connection. She found the letter very curious and showed it to the police, who said it was likely a scam and advised against replying.

Again, on a drive down the mountain from my little Tuscan

village, I reasoned that three weeks was a more than sufficient time to wait and Elaine was not going to reply. I decided I must be more aggressive in my attempt to make contact. My next letter stated the facts, backed up by documentation. I wrote, "Your father was married to my mother. We could be related. Please find enclosed…" and I numbered and itemized my list of enclosed documents: A copy of the marriage certificate between Claudia Faye Gates and Keith Broderick Howard; my birth certificate naming Claudia as my mother; my adoption paper showing my name change from John Robin Howard to Michael Carlson, and Keith's death certificate naming Elaine as respondent.

Just a few days later, it must have been immediately after her receipt of my letter, Elaine phoned me.

"How can I help?" she asked, and hopefully expressed the notion that perhaps I was her brother.

"Do you have an attic in your house," I asked.

"Yes," she replied.

"Go up to the attic and look for any documents," I said.

She did, and what she found was a major piece in the puzzle. She phoned with the news.

"I've found documents. I have his divorce certificate," Elaine said excitedly, "and it names two co-respondents. Are you ready for this? One of the names is Robin Daniel Jacobs."

As soon as I heard the name Robin Daniel, echoing my birth name, John Robin, I knew that had to be it. That was for me a very important moment.

Elaine also found her father's war records, his Dunkirk evacuation certificate, and some wartime photos of him in uniform, all of which proving that Keith, stationed overseas, could not have been my father. She sent me copies.

Once again, I went to the online General Register and requested for one Robin Daniel Jacobs certificates of birth, marriage, divorce and death. Unfortunately, I received them all…

# About my father

Robin Daniel Jacobs.
Born 1908.
Deceased 1977.
The birth certificate named his parents, Ruth and Jonathan Jacobs. The name Jonathan was close enough to the name John, and there it was again – my name, John Robin. One would assume, given their surname, that they were Jewish, and I knew it was customary for Jewish people to name a child after a deceased relative, usually a grandparent. I continued to delve. Not only was Robin Daniel Jacobs mentioned on Claudia's decree absolute (final divorce document), but adultery was also stated as grounds for divorce in the decree absolute of Moyra and Robin Daniel Jacobs. Clearly, there had been something between Robin and Claudia, long term enough for it to have become common knowledge, and serious enough for it to have led to two divorces. I looked up census reports for information on where Robin lived and when, and I applied for and received his military records. Robin Daniel Jacobs was certainly in the right place at the right time to have fathered me.

An important breakthrough came when I looked at an online map and realized that their addresses placed Claudia and Robin around the corner from one another, making them next door neighbors. They could well have shared a shelter during the air raids. In addition, Claudia was listed as working as a waitress and Robin's profession was registered as head waiter. Yet another piece of the puzzle came to light sometime later when I learned via my mother's niece, (more later on how she came into the picture) who had it from her mother that Claudia worked at the Birmingham Small Arms (BSA) company in 1940. Among Robin Jacob's records was evidence that he worked there at the same time. So again, it was clear that opportunity for them to have met, spent time together and formed a relationship was abundant. I felt certain that this man must be my father, this Jewish man. Far from being put off by the thought, I embraced it. That particular association filled me with pride.

I gathered my children and told them, "My father, your grandfather, was Jewish. How do you feel about that? Are you surprised?"

To which my daughter Miriam replied, "After what's been going on for the past few months, Dad, I wouldn't be surprised if you told me your father was an alien." She's always had a wry sense of humour.

If he was Jewish, I reasoned, he probably belonged to a synagogue.

Search and discovery

## **Meeting my family**

I rang Singers Hill Synagogue in Birmingham, told them my story and mentioned the names of those I was looking for. Although the person I spoke with said he didn't know them and couldn't really help, he turned out to be a very great help indeed. He told me about an online service called the Jewish Genealogical Society. He suggested I join and enter the names of those I was looking for. This I did, and the website showed me a match. Caroline Bernstein of Tzfat, Israel, had entered a search request regarding the Jacobs family name a decade earlier. I contacted her.

*Dear Caroline,*          *Date. Wed, 13 Aug 2008 00:45:32 -0500*

*I have recently found out that I am related to the Jacobs in Birmingham. My father was Robin Daniel Jacobs and my grandfather was Jonathan Jacobs who died in Birmingham in 1945.*
*Do you know of any living relatives in England?*
*I would be very grateful to know as I am going to England in a week's time for a short visit.*

*Kind regards,*
*Mike Carlson*

Caroline, originally from the States but whose grandfather, Benjamin Jacobs, had emigrated to Michigan from the UK, answered my mail almost immediately.

*Hi Mike,*
*Our direct Jacobs ancestors were Samuel and Rachel, who left Birmingham and went to London in the early 1900s. They changed their names to "Jakobi". We don't know of any Jacobs that we're related to – just tracing the Jakobi family is hard enough... My grandfather... left England for America in 1918...*

## Lost & Found

*If you find out anything more about your Birmingham origins, please let me know. It's possible that we do have common origins, though pretty far back.*

*Caroline*

As it turned out, it wasn't that far back at all. At the same time that she answered my mail, Caroline also forwarded it to her cousin, Gadi Hirsh, in Ra'anana, Israel, and to her aunt and the family's keeper of genealogical information, Sheryl Applebaum, in Detroit, Michigan with a short note – "Any ideas for him?" I began an ongoing correspondence with both Sheryl and Gadi.

Sheryl, initially reserved in her response, later admitted that she had been somewhat wary of a complete stranger from the other side of the world claiming to be a relation. But she was impressed by the persistence and thoroughness of my search and verified that my findings rang true with her information. We were soon emailing each other regularly.

About the same time, I went to another website called The Genealogist, and there I found a posting from a Cindy Benson, who lived on the Isle of Lewis off the coast of Scotland. She wrote that she had just finished compiling her family tree and apparently found the process so fascinating that she was willing to help anyone else with an interesting background and in particular with a Jewish connection as she had, to research their family tree. By this time I had only reached as far back as Jonathan Jacobs, who I assumed to be my grandfather. Cindy heard my story and took on the job with all seriousness, even travelling to England to augment her research. She was responsible for turning up two relatives in the UK who had also been searching for family connections and who were unknown until then to the rest of the family. Although their surname was Jacobs, they had lost their Jewishness some generations back, but had always suspected its existence. Robert and Harry Jacobs have since become part of the extended family. Their son has travelled to Israel and met their new family members, and the British-Israeli members of the Jacobs clan, Gadi and Miri, met with them in London.

## Meeting my ancestors

At the same time that all this research and online contact was going on, I initiated face-to-face contact as well. Rochelle and I flew to the UK and met with Keith's daughter, Elaine. And so it was that on August 29th, seven months after receiving the news of my adoption, I met the remains of the paternal side of my family.

Driving behind Elaine and her partner, Bob, we followed them to Singers Hill where we all entered the synagogue – a first for the four of us. I had been in email and phone contact with the rabbi and fixed an appointment to see him. He cleared the day for me and took us to The Old Witton Jewish Cemetery where he showed me the graves of my ancestors. "Mike," he said, "this is your grandfather, Jonathan, and this is your great grandmother, Loretta Daniels, the mother of Jonathan and Samuel." He translated the writing on the tombstones for me. Loretta Daniels, my research revealed, was the daughter of Joshua and Miriam Daniels. My breath caught when I encountered that name, Miriam. Without knowing, Rochelle and I had named our daughter after my great-great grandmother. That realization was a very emotional experience.

After saying goodbye to Elaine and Bob, Rochelle and I got back into our car and headed for Manchester, to the cemetery where my father was buried. It was a difficult drive, down a congested motorway. My emotions were in a turmoil after having "met my family." My thoughts were anywhere but on the road. I probably shouldn't have been driving, but we somehow arrived without incident. It was late and we checked into a motel. Bolstered with fish & chips and a bottle of wine, we settled down for dinner in front of the TV, and what should be on… "Who do you think you are?", a program about finding family roots. It featured Jerry Springer, a Jew seeking knowledge of his ancestors. It was very moving, and I couldn't help feeling it was no coincidence, my seeing this program at this moment in time. Jerry Springer even met newfound cousins from Israel, playing out a scenario I was soon to repeat.

The next morning we went to Manchester Southern Cemetery, past the Moslem section and on to the adjacent Jewish section. We had a map and the address of the location of my father's grave. Rochelle saw it first. It wasn't a proper headstone, just what they call an indicator stone. It had fallen over and was lying on the ground. It had but one word written on it – Jacobs. Only in the cemetery records did his full name and details appear. Thus my meeting with my father, at his neglected and tossed aside gravesite, was rather more upsetting than it might have been. Some cemetery workers nearby saw me standing there looking very distraught. They came over and asked if I was alright.

I said, "Look at that!" indicating the stone lying on the ground.

"That's no problem," they said, "we can soon fix that." They dug a slot in the earth, and inserted the stone, fixing it upright. A small thing I could do for my father.

A lot of healing took place that day. I had met as much as I could of my family. Only my father's daughter, Linda Denise Jacobs, who was the respondent on his death certificate, alluded any attempts at being found. Nevertheless, I felt I was getting to the bottom of things, understanding who's who and where I fit in, and I was reconnecting with my Jewish past.

## Dispelling all doubt

I felt quite certain that Robin Jacobs was my paternal parent, but I wanted to dispel all doubt. I wanted proof, and began investigating how best to obtain it. Apparently, I needed a direct male descendant of the Jacobs line. I contacted my Michigan email pal, Caroline's Aunt Sheryl. Sheryl's father and grandfather were both Jacobs and they had been resident in the UK. Sheryl had two brothers. I asked if perhaps one of her brothers would be willing to do a DNA test. It involved only a swab of the inside of the cheek. Yes, she told me, her brother Donald would do the test and send it to the lab I had contacted in the UK. I did the same.

The results came back unequivocal. It was all there in our genes. Donald and I were, without doubt, close relations. Now I had my proof. Proof of belonging. Proof of association. No more stories and no more deception. At last I felt I was truly a member of a wider family.

I had identified my father. I was a Jacobs.

I wrote to Sheryl: *I am very pleased that I have a Jewish father, and although I am not Jewish... I will be very pleased if you can accept me for what I am. I have attached a recent photo of myself and my 18-year-old daughter, Miriam (the joy of my life).*

Looking back, I surprise myself that that's what I wrote. I actually felt Jewish once I found out my father was. I've since been told that the closing words of that particular mail melted any residual reserve Sheryl may have had toward me and from then on she embraced me with all her heart as a newfound cousin.

Similar embraces now became a new and welcome aspect of my life. Caroline had put me in touch with her cousin Gadi, and we began communicating regularly. Originally from London, where he was known as George, he had been living in Israel, just north of Tel Aviv, since 1978. Gadi's mother was Helene Jacobs (prior to the family name change to Jakobi). Based on further research, we worked out that our grandfathers – mine, Gadi's and Sheryl's – were brothers. Caroline, Sheryl's niece, was the next generation.

Reaching out to make the acquaintance of our newfound family, Rochelle and I first met Gadi and his wife, Miri, over Skype. There we were, from our island home off the coast of New Zealand, saying hello to cousins on the other side of the globe, in their home in Israel. From here on things seemed to accelerate rapidly.

Caroline wrote that her eldest son was about to be married and she invited Rochelle and me to the wedding in Israel. It was to be during the summer when we'd be in our Italy home, a mere three-hour flight away. We accepted the invitation. I was excited at the prospect of visiting Israel and meeting Caroline and her family. I wrote to Sheryl in one of our now frequent communications, and told her about my decision. She would have loved to be there as well, but her husband was battling serious illness, so travelling was out of the question. I mentioned that I was a bit nervous, not knowing what to expect or what rules of behaviour I should know about. Sheryl sent me a "kipa" (the traditional small round head covering worn by observant Jews) and told me that was all I needed, and I'd be fine.

Search and discovery

# Touchdown in Israel

Our arrival in Israel aroused a deep emotional reaction. I was returning to a place where my ancestors once lived. I was afloat on the tides of history and destiny was in control.

Gadi and Miri had kindly offered to meet us at the airport, host us in their home, and drive up north with us to Tzfat for the wedding. Bearing in mind we had only ever seen each other on a computer screen, I hoped we'd recognize one another among the tumultuous crowds at Ben Gurion Airport. But once we came through the doors and out into the airport arrivals terminal, we spotted each other with no trouble and from the first, met like old friends. They turned out to be the perfect hosts, easy to get along with, and most important, they were family!

On the drive from the airport to Ra'anana, Gadi, who had lots of experience showing around first-time corporate visitors, kept up a steady stream of explanations as to where we were and what we were seeing. It seemed a vibrant busy place. I was impressed with the level of development I saw, the amount of building going on in central Israel, and the upmarket accommodation in Ra'anana. However, having just arrived from Tuscany, and having lived most of my life in New Zealand, I was slightly disappointed with the scenery. I found it far less dramatic than I'd anticipated.

The drive up north gave me a feel for the very different terrain one finds packed into this small country. We passed the stony Carmel mountains (although they wouldn't qualify as more than gentle bumps in New Zealand) overlooking Haifa Bay, where many survivors of the Holocaust of WWII waded ashore under cover of night. As we moved further north, the elevation of the rolling hills and their greenery increased, and from a winding hilltop road we had our first glimpse of the Sea of Galilee, or the Kinneret, as Israelis call it. A glistening spot of blue in this otherwise arid land, it is the country's main water source, a source of life, whose gentle waves whisper with echoes of Biblical stories.

Finally, we climbed the steep road to Tzfat where we would be spending the next few days.

The heart of Tzfat is a vehicle-free ancient city, a warren of narrow alleyways and cobblestone streets built on various levels of the hilltop and connected by a scattering of stone stairways. Alleys are lined with thick-walled stone buildings, some alleys covered by ancient archways. Coming from our several-hundred-year-old Tuscan village, we felt at home. But there was a very big difference. It seemed that every third building here was a house of prayer, and every one of them was an active hub. Interspersed with the synagogues, were houses where the doors stood open, affording a view of the wares within. Much of the old city had become an artists' quarter featuring galleries displaying paintings, sculptures and pottery. Immigrants and artists, Haredim (the ultra-orthodox) and new wave healers – they all lived side by side, giving the community a decidedly eclectic character marked by a friendly acceptance of everyone. I reacted strongly to the very spiritual atmosphere of Tzfat. It attracted me. I was drawn in and wanted to stay. And this was due in no small measure to the large community of orthodox English-speaking ex-pats who made Rochelle and I feel so welcome.

And then there was the wedding. What are Jewish Israeli weddings like, I wondered. Now I knew – they were wonderful. Set in an old agricultural settlement converted to an events venue, the wedding reception area was an expansive lawn with a decorative sprinkling of antique farming implements. Lovely old trees sheltered numerous buffet tables offering varieties of food and drink from Moroccan pastries to sliced roast beef, Arak to Scotch. Three musicians stood under a tree and filled the air with music. Guests' attire ranged from smart jeans outfits to elegant dresses. Suits and ties were definitely not an Israeli thing. Considering the warm, humid weather that's a most practical fashion decision. However, they were in uniform evidence among the men from the orthodox religious side of the family, including wide brimmed black hats atop bearded faces. Orthodox and secular seemed to mix easily. The ceremony was on the lawn where the groom, flanked by his parents, was led by a group of his fellow male students and friends singing and dancing him up to the chupa, the wedding canopy. There, he was joined by the beautiful, sparkling-eyed bride accompanied by her parents. Various friends and rabbis were invited to read prayers under the canopy. The traditional wedding agreement, the ketuba, was displayed. Speeches, songs, the glass ceremoniously shattered under the groom's foot, and the canopy became the center of a crowd of people waiting to get close enough to give their hugs and congratulations.

Dinner and dancing was in a different area where tables were set up and waiting. Dancing began with the traditional separation between men and women. The men lifted the groom on a chair and danced round with him while the women danced circles around the bride. Later, mixed dancing took over and we all joined in. Sheryl was right – I had my kipa, and I was fine. It was a joyous event – my first of many Jewish celebrations.

# VIII
# The journey to Judaism – Reconnecting to my ancestral roots

If anyone had suggested to me then, on my first visit to Tzfat, that I would be purchasing a home there, I would have replied with a smile, "I don't think so." We were there only briefly and I was disappointed with the scenery and with the lack of cleanliness of the city. On the other hand, I was very impressed with our hosts in Israel and with the wedding. The atmosphere was easy-going and informal. It seems the scales were slowly tipping, without our even noticing, toward a rapid slide culminating in dramatic changes.

I was proud of my newfound Jewish heritage. My Jewish relatives from my father's side were warm and welcoming. I found myself wanting to express my spiritual side, and for the first time I felt I had a framework for doing so. And perhaps coming closer to Judaism was a means of coming closer to my father, honouring his memory. There were many reasons, both in my current situation and in my background that drew me to Judaism, leading me to the path I have chosen today.

I have chosen to be Jewish. I have chosen to follow the historic thread of the Jewish People and become a citizen of Israel under the Law of Return. I have chosen to add a third residence to my lifestyle. And my partner, Rochelle, has made her own choices from her own personal convictions, choices which have prompted some to liken her to the Biblical Ruth: *"...whither thou goest, I will go; and where thou lodgest, I will lodge: thy people shall be my people..."* (Ruth 1:16-17).

Looking back, I can point to several salient moments in my life that were markers along the road to where I am today.

## Early epiphanies

In the 1960's I had a spiritual experience. I had learned Bible stories in Sunday school as a child in the UK, but they had been just stories. Suddenly one evening in New Zealand, many years later, those stories came alive for me. In fact, I feel as though that was the moment when my Jewish soul first came alive. I had had a couple of Vodkas in a pub, but I wasn't at all tipsy. I was talking with Benny, our neighbor who was Jewish. He was a member of the British Israelite Movement, which was born in the mid-to-late 1800s. They believe that the 10 lost tribes of Israel went to Western Europe and Britain. There's even a theory that the British royal family are direct descendants of King David.

While Benny was talking to me, I felt a voice in my head saying "you need God in your life". Never having been a believer before, from that moment on I felt certain that there is a God, and that conviction has never left me. This epiphany prompted me to think back to the Bible stories I had learned, and I experienced another realization – they are not just stories, they are all true accounts. This feeling, this belief, has remained a constant undercurrent in my life, always there in the background.

~

Four years later my employer, Lenny Kravitz, invited me to his son's Bar Mitzva. That was when a rabbi took my hands, looked into my eyes and said, "Shalom". In hindsight, this incident has become prominent in my mind, taking on greater significance. I recently looked for Lenny Kravitz, wanting to tell him the news of my embracing Judaism, but he had passed on, and I spoke with his brother instead.

~

Coming forward in time, on the day that I met the rabbi of Singer's Hill Synagogue, several dramatic events took place within that 24-hour period, events that I look back upon as further milestones in my journey. I was in a synagogue for the first time in my life and not just any synagogue, but the one that my father and grandfather had attended. I encountered whatever remained of the people who were my real family, and I had that extra experience of witnessing Jerry Springer discover his Jewish relatives. Perhaps it wasn't a total healing, but it was certainly progress down that road.

I felt I needed to start doing something about all this, and my first thought was to get a Bible and start reading. On a subsequent visit to the Singer's Hill rabbi, I saw in the synagogue a box full of old books. They were destined for burial – the honour Jews pay to sacred books at the end of their useful lives. I asked the rabbi what I should read, saying I thought I ought to start by reading the Bible. He indicated the box and said, "Help yourself." I took three volumes – a Sidur, or prayer book; the Torah, the five books of Moses; and a canvas-bound volume produced for Jewish soldiers – a combination prayer book and calendar, dated 1939-44, so that they'd know the dates of holidays while serving away from home. All out-of-print books about to be buried, to me they were new treasures. We stayed in Birmingham that night with my adoptive sister, Susan, and her husband. After dinner and wine, I went up to bed with my Bible and started with Genesis. The words leapt out at me. The relevance. The reality. Abraham, your ancestors will enter the land of Israel... wow, I thought, that's me! Those are my ancestors! It was a major turning point.

~

While in New Zealand on our little island, my Scottish friend was helping research the Jewish side of my family. She had put me in touch with someone in Israel, and following our contact, I received a phone call.

"You've been talking to Ron Baruch in the Golan Heights," said a woman identifying herself as Sandra Geller.

Cindy Benson, the Scottish genealogy researcher working through Jewish Genealogical Societies, discovered a common thread with Ron Baruch going back several generations. The brother-in-law of Ron's great-great-grandfather was married to the sister of my great-great-grandfather.

"Ron is my brother," Sandra told me. "He's contacted me about you, and we'd like to meet you."

Thinking she was calling from Auckland or thereabouts, I expected to fix a date for the following week. Instead, I was surprised when in response to my saying, "Yes, I'd like that," she replied, "We'll be round in half an hour." They had booked a holiday home on the island, with the additional motive of meeting me and Rochelle.

We watched them drive up the steep path to our house. Sandra got out of the car, our eyes met and bingo! We connected and I knew we'd be good friends. She and her husband were the first Jewish people we had ever met socially. From here on, Sandra and her husband Larry, genuinely nice people, were an integral part of all the changes we were going through. They broke the ice for us, especially with their invitation to join them for a special evening at the Ray Friedman Center, named after the patron of the Epsom

Girls Grammar School, the top girl's state school our Miriam was attending.

The Center was holding a commemorative evening for ANZAC Day (Australia, New Zealand, Army Corps) and Holocaust Remembrance Day. We took Miriam along and there we were, sitting among 350 Jews. It felt strange. I had accepted my heritage, but this was the first time I was actually in a Jewish setting among Jewish people. I thought we must stick out like sore thumbs, although I think only one person actually did – a tall slim blond German from the embassy was in attendance.

Making us all feel welcome, Sue said there was someone I had to meet – Harvey Baruch, a retired Supreme Court judge from Australia. He was quite short – in fact, it struck me that most of the Jewish people I had seen were fairly short, like me. We compared ancestor notes. I mentioned a Jeremy Daniels in my family tree who was deported for criminal behavior to Tasmania. He matched my story with one of his own of a teenage criminal who had been deported to Australia. I thought that very funny coming from a former Supreme Court judge. Before we parted he said to me, echoing my feelings, "Mike, you have a journey to take. I wish you luck on your journey."

The event started with a singer, after which a man introduced his mother who told the story behind the film we were about to see. It was about a wealthy, well-integrated, German-Jewish family. During the war, the father was sent to Dachau concentration camp. The mother, in a bid for her husband's life, gave herself to a German soldier. Her husband was eventually released from the camp and the couple got as far away as they could, arriving in New Zealand. I remember Miriam sat through it all, wide-eyed. It left a big impression on her, and on all of us. I mark that night as another one of my turning points.

~

## The journey to Judaism – Reconnecting to my ancestral roots

Sandra's husband, Larry, encouraged me to go to synagogue. I began to fly regularly from our home on the island to Auckland on a Friday to attend Sabbath services. Then I took a bigger step and began a year-long conversion course. There were ten of us in the class. I would fly over on Friday or Saturday evening for the 3-hour Sunday lessons.

I had become a weekly commuter from the island to Auckland. After several weeks of this, we decided to rent our house on the Island and locate ourselves in Auckland. Having advertised our needs in the local synagogue newsletter, we were offered a 2-room living space for rent in the home of a wonderful Jewish couple, affording us a glimpse into everyday Jewish life. During our stay there, with occasional Shabbat dinners together, we learned so much about living as Jews, keeping a kosher kitchen and observing the Sabbath.

I found the conversion course in Auckland quite enjoyable and obtained a wealth of books from the Ray Friedman Jewish library. But after a while I felt that the course was not going deep enough to answer my questions. I knew I needed to do something more. It also occurred to me that having discovered and accepted my Jewish ancestry, I wanted to feel that I was also accepted by them. In fact, I wanted to know I would be accepted into Israel as a Jew under the Law of Return.

I spoke with a representative of the Jewish Agency. I needed proof of having a Jewish parent – one was enough. That meant I needed a proper birth certificate that named my father, and I needed proof of his Jewishness. The latter was obtained easily enough in the form of a letter from the rabbi of the Manchester Synagogue where my father attended during his final years, along with a photograph of his gravestone in the Jewish cemetery and the cemetery records. Now I had to tackle the issue of my birth certificate, which turned out to be a daunting task, but I would not be deterred.

## Lost & Found

I spoke to the reform rabbi leading the course, explaining my reasons for being excused. I would be flying to Italy and the UK, where I would be working on obtaining my original birth certificate. While in the UK, I went again to Birmingham and attended the service at Singer's Hill synagogue. I soaked up the atmosphere around me, keenly aware of the fact that my father and my grandfather had been there, perhaps sat on the very seat I was in, or perhaps next to me, breathing the air within these walls. My grandfather attended quite regularly, having lived next door to the synagogue. That service was another turning point for me. The orthodox service felt right. I felt at home with it and I just knew this was the right way.

~

Looking back today, from the safe distance of time, I realize that after receiving the news of my adoption, I went to pieces. The foundation of my identity pulled out from under my feet, emotions in a turmoil, I went downhill fast, feeling lied to, cheated, rejected, and generally depressed. Five months later, after having discovered my Jewish father, I felt that God spoke to me.

Much later, standing before the rabbinical judges of the Bet Din, the Jewish court in Israel, one of the Judges asked me, "All right, so you discovered you were adopted and that your father and his family were all Jewish. So why all this?"

This was how I answered him: "One day as I walked from my bedroom down the hall, I heard a voice in my head – 'you've got a belief, a land, a people, and a language.' That's why, Your Honour. I have a mission to accomplish."

I was inextricably moving in that direction anyway, but now I knew I had to address those four things. At 65, for most people the age of retirement, of relaxing and reflecting, I eagerly looked ahead and embarked on my new life's journey.

## Official recognition – The key to my future

There were two reasons why I had to have a declaration of parentage and a proper, true birth certificate naming my birth parents. The practical reason was that it was required if I was to invoke the Law of Return. A proper birth certificate, naming my true father, was my passport to acceptance into Israel. The second reason, no less compelling, was that I needed it for my own peace of mind, a declaration of my identity, the truth of my birth no longer a hidden secret but recognized and sanctioned.

My first plan of action was to write an affidavit declaring that Robin Daniel Jacobs was my father and to get it signed by Claudia, my birth mother. I asked Margaret, Claudia's youngest daughter who I had met with in London, if she would give such a document to her mother to sign. Margaret refused.

I had no choice but to go through the legal system. I had court papers delivered to my mother by a court process server. In response, Claudia wrote a letter to the judge. In it, she neither denied nor confirmed my contentions as to the identity of my paternal parent, but merely stated that she wanted nothing to do with the case. She had spoken with the process server who later had the conversation transcribed. She stated that there had been a rape, and she therefore did not feel she should be forced to dredge up old unpleasant memories. The one small positive grain I found in all of this, was that she did not once contest the fact that Robin Daniel Jacobs was, in fact, my father. However, her contention that I was the product of rape disturbed me greatly. Given all that we had uncovered about the circumstances, and the lack of any accusations having been made at the time, backed by a police report verifying that no criminal record of any kind existed for Robin Daniel Jacobs, it seemed most unlikely. I did not understand why she made this claim.

What I had to do now was gather and organize all the evidence at my disposal to convince the judge of my paternal parentage, and present it in a petition to the court. I devoted myself totally to this task, as did my helpmate, Rochelle, searching, collecting, collating and filing documents, reports, and any scrap of evidence we could lay our hands on. I also had a very close friend, Carl Sanders, who was a barrister and helped me prepare the court documents. I will always be appreciative of his encouragement to discover the truth, and we remain close friends.

After 18 months of diligent work by myself and Rochelle, the copious file of evidence was ready and sent by courier from New Zealand to the Birmingham District Court, UK. Once it was received and processed, the legal proceedings consisted of five personal appearances in court and one hearing conducted by phone between myself on the New Zealand island and the judge in Birmingham. For this pleasure, I had to pay several hundred pounds to obtain a special secured phone line with a recording function.

## My day in court

Seven days prior to the last hearing on the matter, I flew to the UK to present my case to the court – all 60-plus pages of the tabulated and paginated file including every document and affidavit I'd managed to collect. Representing myself, I saved thousands of pounds sterling on lawyer's fees. I was told this was the first time such a case had been served by a child against the parents. Until then, the court's experience had only been with parents filing to claim parentage.

After a long process of presenting every piece of my evidence, and its meticulous consideration by the judge, the ruling was announced, "I hereby declare that Robin Daniel Jacobs is the Father of Michael Carlson previously known as John Robin Howard."

Upon hearing these words I was so filled with a mix of emotions I felt fit to burst, and tears were the release valve. The Court issued an order to the General Register of Births Marriages and Deaths in the United Kingdom, which in turn issued my Birth Certificate, naming, for the first time, my biological parents. Finally, I was in possession of my true birth certificate. More than just a document, this was the key that opened doors for me. In fact, it was the floodgate that led to a cascade of events. With my new birth certificate, I was now accepted under the Law of Return. Off we went to Israel.

Lost & Found

## A heart-stopping glitch

In a nightmare scenario that robs you of happiness just when it's at its peak, along came another judge and declared that the ruling regarding my parentage was beyond the jurisdiction of the District Court and had to go to the High Court.

Bracing myself for a renewed fight, I booked a flight from Tel Aviv to the UK, and once again found myself in a Birmingham courtroom. Having argued that it was the court's mistake, I was at least released from having to pay another round of court fees. Surprised that I was representing myself, a court clerk asked if I knew what to do. "No, I've never been in a High Court in my life," I replied. He told me to stand when the judge entered the courtroom and gave me other such last minute instructions.

The judge entered, I stood, and then the judge said, "Look, I'm just back from holiday. I haven't had time to read through the very copious material regarding this case. I need more time to read it."

To which I replied, "Your Honour, I'm flying back to New Zealand on Tuesday night."

The judge said, "Alright, come back on Tuesday," and that was the disappointing end of High Court hearing number one.

When I returned on Tuesday, the now well prepared judge said, "This is the most complicated family case I've ever seen," and he proclaimed his ruling: "The Honourable Mr. Justice Callaghan, having read all of the evidence filed by the Applicant Michael Carlson, confirms the order made by District Judge Gainsborough on the 3rd June 2010."

This time, rather than the thrill of delight, my main feeling was one of great relief that my hard won authenticated identity had not been taken from me. I thanked his honour, left the court and returned to Israel.

In all, I had taken part in four District Court hearings and two High Court hearings. My battle was finally finished and won, my true identity acknowledged and documented.

However, there was one more day in court I would demand. The allegation of rape does not at all sit well with me and I intend to have it removed with an official statement. Having been born under awkward circumstances, I would like to hold on to any of its positive aspects, rather than let lie sordid accusations.

## Living in Tzfat

Once I had produced my new birth certificate, it took just six more weeks for my Aliya (immigration into Israel as a Jew) to be approved. I received my Israeli passport six months later. And the words continued to reverberate in my mind: A belief, a land, a people, and a language.

When we were in Italy, I had spoken about converting with Rabbi Levy of Florence, and he advised me to do it in Israel. I was prepared to go through with the conversion on my own. I never pushed Rochelle to do anything. It was understood that I was doing what I felt I needed to do, with no obligation on her part. Nonetheless, Rochelle was instrumental in helping make the decision to go to Israel and spend up to six months there, saying that we'd start out with a few weeks and see how it goes. We may decide to stay longer or not.

Knowing that I'd be undergoing a conversion process to be officially, rabbinically accepted as a Jew, I knew I needed to live near an observant Jew who would 'adopt' us for Sabbaths and holidays. My cousin, Caroline, in Tzfat, was the perfect candidate, and so Tzfat, which we had found intriguing on our first visit, became our chosen destination.

Living in Tzfat was a new experience. Here, one breathes spirituality, is surrounded by it, by Jewishness, all the time. It was in Tzfat that Rochelle began to change too. We quickly integrated into the social fabric of life. There were so many English-speaking orthodox people and they were wonderfully friendly. We had a constant stream of dinner invitations. We became particularly close with Moshe and Gila Horowitz, who had emigrated from the US, although Moshe was originally South African. They had a very strong positive effect on Rochelle and me.

## The journey to Judaism – Reconnecting to my ancestral roots

Our life in Tzfat involved a daily morning walk to Ulpan, the place where new immigrants are transformed into new Israelis. At Ulpan they teach not only the Hebrew language, but about Judaism itself, the customs, the holidays, the songs, and the culture of Israel. At the same time, I was studying two hours a day at a yeshiva (religious college) in Tzfat toward my conversion.

Meanwhile, Rochelle, quietly and on her own, was devouring books supplied by Gila. When I felt ready, I arranged to see Rabbi Gruber, head of conversions for the north of the country, to find out how to proceed. Rochelle said she'd like to see the rabbi with me, which surprised and delighted me. I thought to myself, "Oh, this sounds like another turning point if she wants to see the rabbi, too."

The rabbi agreed to see us both and our interview with him consisted of his asking us, especially Rochelle, heaps of questions testing our knowledge of Judaism. She did very well in answering them all. It was quite a long interview. I had just wanted to know what to do next to become Jewish. I already felt Jewish anyway, but wanted the recognition of being accepted Halachically – according to rabbinical law. This rabbi was the gateway. He would instruct us how to do it.

He asked us personal questions as well as Jewish knowledge questions. Finally, one of the last questions he asked was, "How do you shave?" I thought that rather odd. I answered, "With a razor." He then said, "You'll have to stop that. Either grow a beard like me, or use an electric shaver." Finally he said to me, "You can go buy a talit (a prayer shawl) and tefilin (phylacteries). I'm going to recommend you to the Beit Din." I was in tears when I told my closest Tzfat friend, Moshe.

My final conversion was about to take place. I had worked toward this moment. I had attended a conversion course for four months in Auckland. I had done an online correspondence course with Aish Torah, recommended by my cousin Caroline, and consisting of 1.5 to 2 hours a day of studies, which I did together with Rochelle, sharing whatever I learned. I attended a yeshiva in Tzfat for 2 hours a day over the course of 3-4 months, while Rochelle studied on her own. And finally, we both attended Ulpan for 5 months, passing our written and verbal exams at the end, with Rochelle getting much higher marks than mine! Ulpan had a huge effect on us – it truly was a melting pot, preparing people from all over the world to take up life as Jews in Israel.

We arrived at the Beit Din, the rabbinical court, accompanied by Caroline and Moshe as our proponents. They were invited into the chambers first and questioned. Next, Rochelle and I were invited in together and once again tested on Jewish knowledge by a panel of three rabbis along with Rabbi Gruber. One of the questions regarded why one says Havdala at the end of Shabbat (the prayer distinguishing the sanctity of the Sabbath from ordinary weekdays), and our answer had not been quite right. We were then asked to leave while they deliberated. It was a tense moment – in fact it felt like an eternity.

Finally, we were all invited back in, and were solemnly given the verdict of the rabbinical court: "We have decided to accept you into the Jewish People, but we want you to do three things. Mike, you must be circumcised. Both of you must go to a mikva (a ritual bath). And you must be married under a chupah." Official acceptance achieved, my heart was full.

Six weeks later, with the first and most formidable of our missions accomplished, we went back to Haifa to fill in marriage documents. We were told that from the moment we enter the mikva until our marriage ceremony, we must not have conjugal relations. In fact, given the nature of mission number one, which included some stitches, I couldn't have if I had wanted to. But to be seen to be doing the right thing, we decided that from the mikva and until the wedding, Rochelle would be resident in our rented flat, while I would stay with my cousin Caroline.

Confronting mission number two was next on the agenda. We were a little nervous about our appearance at the mikva. With the understanding that there must be no barrier between our bodies and the cleansing waters of the mikva, we scrubbed thoroughly before setting out – no nail varnish or make-up, no jewelry or hairpins, no creams, sprays or perfumes. There was also a blessing we had to learn and we practiced it diligently.

Our first challenge was to find the place, as mikvas are traditionally unobtrusive and hidden away so that women can keep their ritual monthly cleansing visits discrete. This one was outside of Jerusalem and it was one of the few that dealt with men and women and conversions. Finally detecting its location, we completed the paperwork and each of us went off to separate areas. Once again I showered and donned a robe. The attendant, a kindly lady, took me through the whole process. I found the first ritual bath we approached too hot, so she led me to a different one which was fine. I totally submersed myself three times and recited the blessing. Then the rabbis entered and I repeated the procedure for them, reciting the prayer once again. It all happened quite quickly, but not without a deep feeling of complete satisfaction. I rather enjoyed it. I felt I could stay in there all day, in the warm cleansing waters, especially since the weather outside was nasty and grey.

When Rochelle and I emerged, feeling squeaky and spiritually clean, we had a lovely surprise. There, waiting to greet us, was our own cheering party consisting of Gadi, Miri, and Sheryl, throwing sweets at us and shouting mazal tov. What an auspicious, first face-to-face meeting this was with Sheryl, after having communicated online for nearly 4 years. When she heard about our approaching wedding she felt she had to be there. Her husband, sadly, had passed away by this time. Making the quickest travel decision of her life, she hopped on a plane and gave us a wonderful surprise with her presence in Israel. We sat together at a nearby café and then drove to Gadi and Miri's home in Ra'anana for a celebratory feast.

Later that evening, as I drove back to Tzfat, I reflected on the very emotional experience of the day. I felt that this was the real reason I had been confronted with the fact of my adoption. It was so that I could reconnect with my heritage. It all led to my becoming a Jew. And now, save for the Jewish wedding ceremony to take place in a few days' time, it was all done. I not only felt a genuine member of my Jewish family, but I was now accepted as a member of a very large family indeed. A well satisfied Mike drove home toward Tzfat that night.

I was surprised the next day by a phone call from the Prime Minister's Office in Jerusalem. The Prime Minister's secretary said they had heard about our story and wanted to offer their congratulations, and that if we were willing, they would send a reporter and cameras to the wedding. As soon as I was sufficiently recovered from the shock of the call, I asked the Prime Minister's secretary if she would kindly extend our invitation to the wedding to her boss. She replied that he was a very busy man, but promised to convey our invitation. The Prime Minister never turned up, but the day after the wedding we were headline news with a full page and photo in Israel's largest circulation daily paper.

## The wedding

Rochelle's sister, Pamela, arrived from London. Gadi and Miri collected her from the airport and brought her and Sheryl up to Tzfat for the event. Caroline and her five children were all in attendance at this our second, our Jewish wedding, along with 60 or so of our friends from Tzfat, one of whom had provided his home as the wedding venue.

Rochelle, in her new white dress and borrowed angora bolero, was as beautiful a bride as she had been some 30 years before. And I'm told I looked quite dapper in my new suit and overcoat. A friend of a friend played his fiddle and another the guitar. Between them they kept the music going all evening. The wedding ceremony was out back in the courtyard making the "walk down the aisle" a dramatic appearance through the doorway of the home. The ceremony under the chupah, the lovely wedding canopy; displaying the ketuba, the traditional wedding contract; stamping on the glass, the rabbis' prayers, the joyous dancing afterwards, our cousins pointing cameras recording the event, row upon row of tables and well-wishing diners – it all blended into a blur of happiness and fulfillment. Our conversion was now accomplished and I was well and truly reconnected with my roots. The feeling of belonging that I never had, was complete.

# IX
# An expanding family

By now I had discovered and met quite a number of my family members, to greater or lesser degrees of delight on their part. Among my mother's children, I maintain contact with Margaret and sporadic contact with Harriet, while Charles, being a very obedient son, has declined all contact, as has my mother herself. However, every other family connection I have uncovered has proved to be warmly welcoming. Oddly enough, it was a relation on my father's side that led to my discovery of another cousin from my mother's side who has proved to be a most significant source of information, as well as a genuine friend with whom I enjoy increasingly close contact. It happened like this.

I met Gerald Stevenson on my first trip to Israel. He was one of the guests who arrived with his family from the US for Caroline's son's wedding. All the overseas guests were ensconced over the weekend in the dormitories of Livnot, the Tzfat-based organization Caroline worked for that brought young people to Israel for a Jewish-Israeli experience based on the organization's name – Livnot u'Lehivanot, literally translated, to build and be built. Thus we had ample opportunity to mingle and get to know one another. Gerald and I had some long conversations, during which he learned about my family and my saga. We kept in contact after that.

Back in the States, Gerald was putting together his own family tree through Ancestry.com and he added whatever he

## An expanding family

had learned about my parentage to his tree. The website had a Members Connect option, and that's when the two sides of my family collided. Detecting a name in common – Claudia Faye Gates – it linked Gerald Stevenson with a woman related to my mother. Her name was Jeanette Hathaway. When Gerald received an email from Jeanette asking, "Why do you have my Aunt Claudia on your family tree?" he immediately contacted me, "Mike, I think you'd better get in touch with this woman." I called her, we spoke and it was an instant mutual like.

Jeanette is a Magistrate in the UK. Whereas other relatives on my mother's side seemed timid about looking too closely at things, Jeanette was far more confrontational. In fact, she was all for confronting my mother, whom she described as a drama queen. And she began to shed light on my mother's childhood. She told me that whenever she asked her father, Claudia's younger brother, about his childhood, he would begin to talk about it and soon after start to cry, saying he couldn't go on. He didn't want to remember. What she managed to understand from him was that their father would often come home drunk, and when he did, he would beat his sons.

## Horrific revelations

A mother giving up her child for adoption is not a natural course of events. It is an aberrant occurrence. Any adopted person seeking knowledge of their background and the circumstances of their birth must be prepared for the discovery of events involving anything from heartbreak to criminal abuse. I understood this. I thought I was prepared, but I found I was most unprepared for the next chapter of revelations.

The story came out piece by piece, as Jeanette and I communicated from one side of the world to the other, she in the UK, me in New Zealand (we did eventually meet, in the UK, and again in Tuscany where we plan to get together when Jeanette and her husband visit their recently purchased holiday home not far from ours). She questioned her father as much as she was able without distressing him unduly. She questioned her cousins, and she delved into historical records. Before he cut off contact with me, Charles had said that something terrible happened to his mother when she was a girl. Two days later, at the first meeting with my sister Margaret, she remarked that our mother's father was "a very evil man." At the time, I dared not put the two statements together. But now, long hidden skeletons came tumbling out of the closet when Jeanette uncovered a news item from 1937. The article, headed *Five Years' Penal Servitude,* read simply: *Eli Gates (47) an electrical engineer, pleaded guilty to a serious offence against his daughter, a girl of fourteen, and was sentenced to five years' penal servitude.*

More than 70 years later, the unmentionable, the terrible secret was out. Further enquiries confirmed that Claudia had borne a child from her father at the age of 14. It was given up for adoption, disposed of and forgotten. Now, finally, I understood my mother's reluctance for contact. I understood her claim of rape. In her 80's, she perhaps confused or linked the two

## An expanding family

past events. Twice, she had borne and given up an illegitimate child. When it happened a second time, although under very different circumstances, the solution had already been tried and proven. Now, confronting one event meant recalling the other. And given the circumstances of the first, one can understand her horror at the thought of confronting the product of her despoiler, the man who should have been her father and protector but was instead her criminally abusive demon. Can I blame her for not wanting to come face to face with her childhood nightmare? I can now make some sense of my mother's reaction. I can be compassionate. I can, perhaps, forgive her.

# X
# From here on...

I came into the world as John Robin Howard. I grew up as Mike Carlson. Today I am Mike (or to my friends in Tzfat, Yonatan) Jacobs, and at peace with who I am.

It is perhaps a reflection of who I am now, that I divide myself among three different homes. They express the different parts of me. I fell in love with New Zealand as a boy, grew up there and lived my adult life there. New Zealand will always feel like home. But I also have my home-away-from-home, our family-owned villa in Tuscany where we delight in growing our own vegetables and drinking home-made wine, reveling in the lush scenery and sharing the simple life of the villagers. And now, there's my spiritual home in Tzfat, Israel, where I feel a deep sense of belonging, satisfaction and contentment as we begin furnishing our newly built apartment and dedicate a corner of our balcony to the exciting enterprise of fermenting our first batch of hand-picked grapes, soon to become our homemade Israeli wine. From the expansive balcony we can see the distant glistening of the Sea of Galilee. We look forward to filling the balcony with greenery and guests.

Five years after the emotional earthquake set off by the discovery of my adoption, a discovery that left me feeling lost and questioning my own identity, I have come full circle, integrating who I was then with who I am now. I have found my identity, my roots, and as a result our life's landscape has

## From here on…

changed, becoming enriched and expanded. The new connection to my real family is something I never had before. Perhaps that was the reason I needed to discover the fact of my adoption and the truth of my origins. The task was not an easy one. It was costly and emotionally draining. But I would not for one second have done otherwise. In the end, dogged perseverance won out. I am comfortable with the truth. I might even, with encouragement and prodding from Jeanette, pop in and see my mother one day. The road ahead continues to evolve and I now travel it with a new inner peace.